IMAGES
of Sport

KENT

COUNTY CRICKET CLUB

KENT.

2

IMAGES
of Sport

KENT
COUNTY CRICKET CLUB

Compiled by
William A. Powell

TEMPUS

Tempus Publishing Limited
The Mill, Brimscombe Port,
Stroud, Gloucestershire, GL5 2QG

ISBN 0 7524 1871 8

Typesetting and origination by
Tempus Publishing Limited
Printed in Great Britain by
Midway Clark Printing, Wiltshire

Also available from Tempus Publishing

Glamorgan CCC	Andrew Hignell	0 7524 0792 9
Glamorgan CCC 2	Andrew Hignell	0 7524 1137 3
Glamorgan Greats	Andrew Hignell	0 7524 1879 3
Hampshire CCC	Hampshire Cricket Museum	0 7524 1876 9
Leicestershire CCC	Dennis Lambert	0 7524 1864 5
Scarborough Festival	William A. Powell	0 7524 1638 3
Somerset CCC	Somerset Cricket Museum	0 7524 1585 9
Worcestershire CCC	Les Hatton	0 7524 1834 9
Yorkshire CCC	Mick Pope	0 7524 0756 2
Charlton FC	David Ramzan	0 7524 1504 2
Crystal Palace FC	Nigel Sands	0 7524 1544 1
Final Tie	Norman Shiel	0 7524 1669 3
Gillingham FC	Roger Triggs	0 7524 1567 0
Gillingham Greats	Roger Triggs	Summer 2000
Millwall FC 1885-1939	Millwall FC Museum	0 7524 1849 1
QPR	Tony Williamson	0 7524 1604 9
Blackheath Rugby Club	Dave Hammond	0 7524 1688 X
The Five Nations Story	David Hands	0 7524 1851 3

(all books are 128 page softbacks with the exception of *The Five Nations Story* which is a 176 page hardback with colour illustrations.)

Contents

Foreword

Kent cricket is rich in history and I congratulate William Powell for putting together this fascinating pictorial record. What a remarkable tapestry of interesting Kentish folk he is able to weave together, thus reviving our memories.

I cannot help wondering if we ever had two better cricketers than Alfred Mynn and Fuller Pilch. We shall never know, but that great Kent XI, pre-Hambledon, who beat everyone (including the All England XI of the day) was every bit as good as the 1906 Championship winning side – I wonder how it would have fared against the Kent XI of the 1970s!

The sequence of outstanding captains reminds us of how lucky we have been. Lord Harris was a fine batsman and athlete in his own right, who enjoyed fifteen years leading the side. He was everything to Kent cricket, not just during that span, but throughout his lifetime; I doubt whether Kent would have been quite so prominent but for the stamp of his personality and love of the game. The J.R. Mason years were also a highlight, and it is just so disappointing that the First World War brought an end to this most successful period of Kent cricket. It is sadder still that we should have lost the life of Colin Blythe at the height of his powers, surely one of the three greatest slow left arm bowlers in the history of the game.

After the Stanley Cornwallis years, A.P.F. Chapman became a huge figure on the Kent and England stage and no wonder the lovely Kent grounds were filled to overflowing when he led a side containing Frank Woolley, Leslie Ames and Tich Freeman. There were so many brilliant amateur cricketers worthy of their places, but spare a thought for those superb professionals who had to be eased out of the side to make way for them in August. I think of Bill Ashdown, a fine opening bowler and dashing opening batsman who scored 300 in a day at the Crabble Ground, Dover, and yet he was a Kent professional in the wings as he waited ten years to play in his first Canterbury Cricket Festival week.

One of our finest captains was Bryan Valentine, a footballer and lawn tennis player of the highest class and a fierce competitor who led Kent with much *joie de vivre*. He surely would have had a longer reign as captain of Kent, and England too, but for the seven years of the Second World War.

I had the privilege of being captain of Kent for fifteen years that embraced so many exciting players, not least Mike Denness, Brian Luckhurst, Alan Knott and Derek Underwood, as well as outstanding overseas players, John Shepherd and Asif Iqbal. We applaud Mike Denness, also an England captain, for it was under his leadership that Kent had its most successful spell, picking up nine trophies.

The leg spinners have been a speciality: Douglas Carr, Tich Freeman, Father Marriott and, of course, Douglas Wright. However, most of all Kent is famous for the wicketkeepers – Huish, Jack Hubble, Hopper Levett, Godfrey Evans and Alan Knott – and let us not forget the more recent performances of Steve Marsh. What is it about Kent that has produced so many good 'keepers – the hopfields, the fruit orchards, the air coming in over the white cliffs of Dover? It is, I believe, more to do with the patriotic fervour and warm spirit of the Men of Kent and Kentish Men, and this lovely book goes a long way to capturing the spirit of Kent cricket.

Lord Cowdrey of Tonbridge CBE
Angmering Park, Littlehampton, West Sussex
February 2000

Introduction

The story of Kent is the story of cricket. Long before the marriage of the Canterbury and Maidstone clubs produced the offspring of the county cricket club in 1870, the famous Kent XI were hailed as the champions within the growing game. In 1744 Kent were powerful enough to take on an All England XI. Three years later they played three matches against England and beat them every time. Kent were Hambledon's most serious rivals, and many were the epic struggles with arch-rivals Surrey.

The Canterbury Cricket Festival, the father of all cricket weeks, began in 1842 and, on the present St Lawrence Cricket Ground, in 1847. The beautiful game with the beautiful name now had its most beautiful setting. A county's style and character is often the reflection of its environment, and, amid the marquees, tents and flowers of Canterbury, Maidstone, Tunbridge Wells, Dartford and Folkestone, Kent have paraded a glittering host of top-class players. From Alfred Mynn, the first of cricket's heroes, Fuller Pilch and Felix (whose real name was Nicholas Wanostrocht), to J.R. Mason, A.P.F. Chapman, Frank Woolley, Leslie Ames, Doug Wright, Godfrey Evans, Colin Cowdrey, Derek Underwood, Alan Knott, Asif Iqbal, Terry Alderman, Carl Hooper, Aravinda de Silva and the Australian Andrew Symonds, Kent have had actors to do honour to their stage.

For sixty years Kent was dominated by the powerful personality of the Fourth Lord Harris, a formidable autocrat of the old school and a pillar of the establishment. He captained Kent from 1871 to 1889, England in Australia in 1878/79 and in the first home Test of 1880, was chairman, president and secretary of Kent County Cricket Club, and president and honorary treasurer of MCC. Apart from spells as Governor of Bombay, under-secretary for India and under-secretary for war, his life was devoted to the game of cricket. He ruled both amateur and professional strictly but with impartiality. Only Lord Harris could have sent a dismissal notice to a wretched bowler halfway through an over in a county match!

A dependence on amateurs often led to erratic results and one of the most significant events – matched later only by the alliance of Leslie Ames and Colin Cowdrey – was the setting-up of the Tonbridge nursery in 1897, which supplied a stream of high quality professionals and more settled sides. The products included Frank Woolley, 'Tich' Freeman, Humphries, Fielder, Seymour, Jack Hubble the wicketkeeper – a position always in safe hands in Kent – and Fairservice. At last Kent were county champions in 1906 (Frank Woolley's first season) and then again in 1909, 1910 and 1913. In between these triumphs they were twice second and once third.

Apart from J.R. Mason, the bowling was professional, headed by Fielder (fast) and Blythe (classical slow left-arm) and the batting mainly amateur and aggressive. Fielder's extra celebration in 1906 was to take all 10 Gentlemen wickets and in the following tour of Australia he had 25 wickets to his name in the series. In the sixteen seasons until he joined up in August 1914, never to return, Colin Blythe took 2,506 wickets, and in his last three seasons he headed the national averages. A violinist, he was of such a sensitive nature that he was forbidden by doctors to play in Test cricket after he had taken 100 wickets in 19 matches at an average of only 18.63. A memorial to this much-loved cricketer stands within the St Lawrence Ground, Canterbury.

With Colin Blythe and Frank Woolley together, Kent enjoyed unrivalled spin. It is hard to credit that a batsman of such elegant flair to be compared with Australia's Victor Trumper and scorer of 58,969 runs and 145 hundreds – an aggregate of runs exceeded only by Jack Hobbs – was in the upper tier of slow left-arm bowlers. Yet Woolley gave up bowling at the age of thirty-five with 2,068 wickets, twelve more than Doug Wright – a statistic designed not to belittle Doug Wright (an unlucky genius) but to underline Woolley's contributions. A cast-off line is his 1,018 catches, a comfortable record. Bowlers of the class of Tate and Constantine confessed they could not bowl to the tall willowy figure, such was the range and invention of his strokes, nor curb his aggressive approach. On no fewer than thirty-five occasions he was out between ninety and ninety-five. 'I never gave a thought to the nervous nineties' he said on his retirement in 1938. 'We were never allowed to play for averages in Kent sides.'

Leslie Ames played in 47 Test matches to Woolley's 64, and maintained the fashion of wicketkeeper-batsman. In both departments Ames was remarkably successful, scoring 102 centuries and bagging 1,121 victims behind the stumps. The combination of Leslie Ames and Tich Freeman, the 5ft 2in leg spinner, whose aggregate was bettered only by Wilfred Rhodes of Yorkshire, was irresistible, but Kent owed as much to Ames the secretary-manager as Ames the player.

Kent had often been in the hunt between the wars, but were too inconsistent to unseat Yorkshire, and from 1946 there were more disappointments than successes. The halcyon years seemed to belong to a long-distant past, but a new dawn broke in 1957 when the new county captain Colin Cowdrey linked with Ames to form a formidable partnership at the helm of Kent cricket.

A brilliant era began with the winning of the Gillette Cup in 1967 when Somerset were defeated at Lord's. That year and the next Kent were runners-up and, appropriately, in 1970, the club's centenary year, the County Championship title went to Cowdrey's men – a remarkable achievement as they were at the foot of the table on 1 July. Kent were in the thick of all the competitions, sharing the title with Middlesex under the leadership of Pakistani Asif Iqbal in 1977. In the following season (1978) Alan Ealham, a superb fieldsman who had taken over the captaincy from Asif Iqbal (then with the Packer circus in Australia), and his side did even better, winning the County Championship and the Benson & Hedges Cup for the third time.

Mike Denness, the Scot who captained England, had five years as Colin Cowdrey's successor, twice leading the county to both the Sunday League and the Benson & Hedges Cup in the same season. He also took the Sunday League and the runners-up position in the County Championship in 1972. Six other appearances in Lord's finals between 1971 and 1996 were further proof of the county's brilliant adoption of single-innings cricket.

There have been few better batsmen than Colin Cowdrey – at his best perhaps another Wally Hammond – and he ended his distinguished career with a record 114 Test caps, 22 centuries for England and having rekindled Kent's pride. Moreover, he saw his son, Christopher, carry the torch as captain of Kent and England. Colin Cowdrey, Doug Wright, Godfrey Evans, Alan Knott (who added 5 Test match centuries to his wicketkeeping prowess) and Derek Underwood (2,465 wickets, including 297 for England), more than upheld the standards set by Kent titans of bygone days.

Having finished runners-up in the County Championship in 1988, Kent slumped to fifteenth in 1989 and sixteenth in 1990. With the introduction of Daryl Foster, the Western Australia coach, the position improved greatly to sixth place in 1991. Mark Benson took over the captaincy from Christopher Cowdrey in 1991 and he led the county to second place in 1992. In 1993 Kent slipped to eighth, a year later to ninth and in 1995 to eighteenth place – the lowest position the club had ever been in the County Championship. Since then things have improved greatly with fourth position in 1996 and second in 1997 under the leadership of wicketkeeper Steve Marsh.

The Sunday League was achieved outright in 1995 and two Benson & Hedges finals were reached in 1995 and 1997, where the county were defeated on both occasions. A minor disappointment in 1998 under the watchful eye of coach John Wright, the former Derbyshire and New Zealand opening batsman, saw the county finish in eleventh place. A year later in 1999, under the leadership of Matthew Fleming in his first season at the helm, Kent finished fifth in the County Championship and third in the CGU Sunday League Division One, thus achieving Championship Division One status for the 2000 season. The close season has already seen the arrival of Indian Test batsman Rahul Dravid and wicketkeeper Paul Nixon from Leicestershire.

This introduction cannot be concluded without my thanking firstly Lord Cowdrey of Tonbridge, the President of the Club for 2000, for his foreword and secondly the many who have assisted me with this work – all those who have made some contribution are included in the acknowledgements. For current players, all statistics are up to and including the end of the 1999 English season.

William A. Powell
Hemel Hempstead, Hertfordshire
February 2000

Kent favourites pose together, from left to right: L.E.G. Ames, C. Wright, W.H. Ashdown, L.J. Todd.

Acknowledgements

The author would like to thank the following, who have assisted in a variety of ways in the preparation of this book: Lord Cowdrey of Tonbridge CBE, Vic Lewis, Peter W.G. Powell, Sohail Malik, Alex Bannister, Diana Walsh, Dora Hall-Newman, John Eastwood, Brian Croudy, Martin Wood, David and Gill Robertson, Wendy Wimbush, the late E.W. 'Jim' Swanton, Carl Openshaw, Giles Lyon, James Howarth, David Buxton, Mike Smith, Bernard Thompson, Brian Luckhurst, Paul Millman, John Newport, Christopher Taylor, John Evans, Kent County Cricket Club players, officials and staff and Kent County Library Service – including Canterbury, Dover, Deal and Folkestone libraries.

I acknowledge the sources of the illustrations, which are many and include the Vic Lewis Collection, *Kent Messenger*, Central Press and Sport & General, Terry Mahoney Photographic Services, Kent County Cricket Club, Tom Morris, Associated Sports Photography, County Print Services, Mike Tarr, Ken Taylor, J.A. Jennings, The Canterbury Printers Limited, Pamlin Prints, Stamp Publicity (Worthing) Limited, Benham, Gillette Limited, Bill Smith, *Yorkshire Evening Post*, Barratt & Co., Odhams Press Limited, B.C. Flemons, Halksworth Wheeler, Charles Harris, J. Mockford, Death & Dunk, Force Cricket Bats, Wisteria Books, H.J. Goulden, R. Scott, Lankesters and W.A. & A.C. Churchman. Apologies are offered to anyone whose photographs have inadvertently been used without acknowledgement.

Nevill Cricket Ground, Tunbridge Wells, 1906.

Bibliography

Kent Cricket: A Photographic History 1744-1984 by E.W. Swanton and C.H. Taylor; Kent County Cricket Club Yearbook 1945 to 1999; Kent County Cricket Club members newsletters; Kent County Cricket Club by Dudley Moore (first and second editions); Kent Cricket Records 1815-1993 compiled by Howard Milton; Kent County Cricket Club Centenary Appeal 1870-1970; Cricket Grounds of Kent by Howard Milton (1992); Kent: The Glory Years by Dennis Fowle (1973); The History of Kent County Cricket by Lord Harris (volume one); The History of Kent County Cricket by Kent CCC (volume two, being appendices F, G, H and I); Kent Cricketing Greats by Dean Hayes (1993); The Story of the Canterbury Cricket Week by H.W. Warner; The Story of the Canterbury Cricket Week: 150 Years 1842-1992 by C.H. Taylor; The Wisden Guide To Cricket Grounds by William Powell (1992).

One
Early Days

Early cricket at Sevenoaks, Kent, in 1780.

The Third Duke of Dorset (1745-1799), one of the county's early patrons.

An amateur, born in Headcorn in 1777, John Willes is depicted here in silhouette from the collection of Ashley-Cooper. He represented Kent between 1815 and 1822, during which time he played 2 matches, took 3 wickets and scored no runs. He died at Staunton near Gloucester in 1852.

Fuller Pilch was born in Horningtoft, Norfolk, in 1804 and he represented the county between 1836 and 1854, scoring 2,844 runs (av. 19.61) with a top score of 98 in 84 matches for the county. He also took 2 wickets (av. 36.00) and held 45 catches. He died of dropsy in Lower Bridge Street in 1870 and is buried in the cemetery adjacent to the Church of St Gregory in Canterbury.

Representing Kent in 90 matches between 1834 and 1859, Alfred Mynn was born in Gouldhurst in 1807. He scored 1,971 runs (av. 12.71) with a top score of 92, bagged 107 wickets (av. 10.20) and held 56 catches. He died in 1861 in Southwark, London.

Kent CCC, 1876. From left to right, back row: E. Henty, G.G. Hearne, H.S. Thomson, W.B. Pattisson, W. Foord-Kelcey, F. Penn, F.A. Mackinnon, V.K. Shaw. Front row: W. Yardley, Lord Harris (captain), C.A. Absolom, Major R.E. Fellows. They played 10 matches during the season with 4 wins and 6 defeats. The 1876 season saw MCC score a record 557 for 9 at Canterbury, which included cricket legend W.G. Grace's ground record innings of 344.

Kent CCC, 1882. From left to right, back row: J. Wootton, G.G. Hearne, Hon. Ivo Bligh, R.S. Jones, C. Wilson, F. Lipscomb. Front row: E.F.S. Tylecote, F.A. Mackinnon, Lord Harris (captain), W. Foord-Kelcey, M.C. Kemp, W.H. Patterson. Having played 9 matches, they finished the season with 2 wins, 6 defeats and a draw.

William Yardley was born in Bombay, India, in 1849 and he played 34 matches for Kent between 1868 and 1878. He recorded 1,473 runs (av. 24.55) with a top score of 126 not out versus W.G. Grace's XI at Maidstone in 1871. He took only 7 wickets, at an average of 18.00 with a best performance of 2-10, and held 20 catches. He died at Kingston-upon-Thames in 1900.

Kent CCC, 1884. From left to right, back row: J. Wootton, H. Hearne, J. Pentecost, G.G. Hearne. Middle row: A.C. Gibson, C. Wilson, Lord Harris (captain), S. Christopherson, F. Marchant. Front row: L. Wilson, F. Hearne. Kent played 16 matches during the season with 7 wins, 7 defeats and 2 draws. County caps were awarded to S. Christopherson and F. Lipscomb.

Kent CCC, 1891. From left to right, back row: F.M. Atkins, A. Daffen, G.G. Hearne, F. Martin. Middle row: W. Rashleigh, F. Marchant, W.H. Patterson, L. Wilson, C.J.M. Fox. Front row: W. Wright, A. Hearne. Kent finished in fifth place in the County Championship (nine teams took part in the competition) having played 15 matches with 4 wins, 5 defeats and 6 draws. F. Marchant and W.H. Patterson shared the captaincy of the county during the season.

Born at Westminster in 1859, the Hon. Ivo Bligh, who became the eighth Earl of Darnley in 1900, was a tall, stylish batsman and a fine fielder. He made his first-class debut for Kent in 1877, scoring a total of 1,493 runs (av. 18.89) with a top score of 105. He also played for Cambridge University between 1878 and 1881 when he gained a blue as a freshman and represented the university when they beat the touring Australians in 1878 by an innings. He led the first England team that recovered The Ashes in 1882/83, after they had been created during a mock obituary following the defeat at Kennington Oval in August 1882. His England side of 1882/83 became the first team to play Ceylon when their ship docked at Colombo en-route to Australia. He played all four of his Tests in Australia, scoring 62 runs at an average of 10.33 with a top score of 19 at Sydney and held 7 catches. He represented the Cambridge Crusaders CC while at university and after his death in 1927 his widow presented The Ashes urn to the MCC Museum.

Kent CCC, 1895. From left to right, back row: W. Bradley, G.J. Mordaunt, J.R. Mason, H.C. Stewart, J. Crowe. Middle row: N. Wright, M.C. Kemp, F. Marchant (captain), H. Patterson, F. Martin. Front row: J.W. Easby, A. Hearne. Kent finished in fourteenth place in the County Championship, having played 18 matches during the season, with 3 wins, 11 defeats and 4 draws. County caps were awarded during the season to W.M. Bradley, J.W. Easby and C.J. Mordaunt.

Kent CCC, 1896. From left to right, back row: W. Wright, F. Martin, Crow (scorer), E.B. Shine, F.H. Huish. Middle row: J.R. Mason, W. Rashleigh, F. Marchant, W.H. Patterson, G.J.V. Weigall. Front row: C.J. Burnup, A. Hearne. Kent finished the season in ninth position, having played 18 matches with 5 wins, 9 defeats and 4 draws. Players receiving county caps during the season included C.J. Burnup, F.H. Huish and E.B. Shine.

Six amateurs from the 1887 team. From left to right, back row: W.H. Patterson, L. Wilson, F. Marchant. Middle row: Lord Harris (captain), M.C. Kemp. Front row: W. Rashleigh. Kent played 14 matches during the season with 1 win, 8 defeats and 5 draws. During the season Yorkshire hit an innings total of 559 at Canterbury, which was the highest recorded by the White Rose County against Kent.

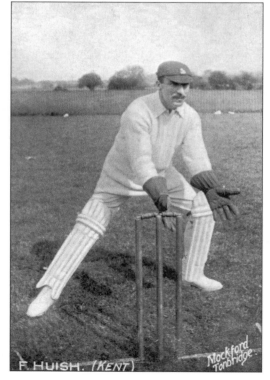

A wicketkeeper-batsman born in Clapham in 1869, Fred Huish represented Kent between 1895 and 1914 in 469 matches, during which time he amassed 901 catches and took 352 stumpings. He also hit 7,247 runs (av. 12.84) with a highest individual innings of 93. He died at Northiam in 1957.

F. HUISH. (KENT)

Mockford Tonbridge.

Born in Trinidad in 1851, when his father was governor there, Lord Harris captained Eton to victory versus Harrow at Lord's in 1870 and later that season he began his sixty-year association with the county, making his Kent debut against MCC at Canterbury. While at Oxford University he attained four blues between 1871 and 1874 and, during 1872, he toured Canada with R.A. Fitzgerald's team. In 1875 he was appointed club president, captain and secretary. Lord Harris took a side to Australia in 1878/79, when he took it upon himself to end the Anglo-Australian cricket crisis. In 1882 he made his highest score of 176 versus Sussex at Gravesend. Playing 157 matches for Kent, he scored 7,842 runs (av. 30.04) with 10 centuries, took 64 wickets (av. 23.79) and he held 155 catches. Later, as the governor of Bombay, he organised the first English tour to India and he fought in the Boer War. Playing in 4 Test matches, he was also the oldest man to play first-class cricket at 60 years 151 days for Kent versus All India at Catford in 1911.

Born in Blackheath in 1875, Cuthbert James Burnup attended Malvern School and Cambridge University between 1895 and 1898, winning blues in 1896, 1897 and 1898 as a sound top-order, right-handed batsman, slow right-arm bowler and good fieldsman. He represented the county in 157 matches between 1896 and 1907, scoring 9,668 runs (av. 38.06) with a top score of 200 versus Lancashire at Old Trafford in 1900. He took 41 wickets (av. 43.78) with a best performance of 5 for 44 and held 74 catches. Burnup also represented London County under W.G. Grace in 1901 and toured abroad with Plum Warner in 1898 and Lord Hawke in 1902/03. He died in Golders Green, London, in 1960.

Representing the county between 1884 and 1906 in 403 matches, top-order, right-handed batsman Alec Hearne was born in Ealing in 1863. He scored 13,598 runs (av. 21.79) with a top score of 94. As a bowler he bagged 1,018 wickets (av. 19.96) with a best haul of 8 for 15 versus Gloucestershire at Tonbridge in 1903 and held a total of 352 catches. He died in Beckenham in 1952.

Kent CCC, 1897. From left to right, back row: E.B. Shine, Hon. J.R. Tufton, F. Martin, F.H. Huish. Middle row: H.C. Stewart, Revd W. Rashleigh, F. Marchant, J.R. Mason, G.J.V. Weigall. Front row: A. Hearne, W. Wright. Kent played 18 matches during the season with 2 wins, 6 draws and 10 defeats. They finished the County Championship in twelfth position with S.H. Day (av. 35.10) and F. Marchant (av. 19.10) top of the batting and bowling averages respectively.

Kent CCC, 1900. From left to right, back row: H.T.W. Hardinge, J. Seymour, C. Blythe, A. Fielder, K.L. Hutchings, W.J. Fairservice. Front row: A. Hearne, E.W. Dillon, C.J. Burnup, S.H. Day, F.H. Huish. Kent finished in equal third place in the County Championship. They played 21 matches during the season with 7 wins, 4 defeats and 10 draws.

Kent CCC, 1905. From left to right, back row: A.P. Day, W.J. Fairservice, A. Fielder, C. Blythe, E. Humphreys, J.C. Hubble. Front row: J. Seymour, F.H. Huish, E.W. Dillon, C.H.B. Marsham (captain), F. Penn, A. Hearne. Kent finished in sixth place in the County Championship, having played 22 matches with 10 wins, 7 defeats, 4 draws and a tied match. During the season Worcestershire recorded their highest innings total in a first-class match against Kent when they amassed 627 for 9 declared at Worcester.

Kent cricketers' autographs, 1890 to 1910. This interesting collection includes C.H.B. Marsham, K.L. Hutchings, A.P. Day, J.C. Hubble, F.E. Woolley, H.T.W. Hardinge, George Hearne, Walter Hearne, Alec Hearne, C. Blythe, E. Humphreys, J.R. Mason, F.H. Huish, W.B. Bradley and C.J. Burnup.

Two
The Golden Age

Kent CCC, taken at Dean Park prior to the County Championship match with Hampshire in 1906. From left to right, back row: F.E. Woolley, F.H. Huish, W. Hearne (scorer), A. Fielder, C. Blythe. Middle row: C.J. Burnup, R.N.R. Blaker, C.H.B. Marsham (captain), K.L. Hutchings, J.R. Mason. Front row: W.J. Fairservice, E. Humphreys, A. Hearne, J. Seymour. Kent finished first in the County Championship, thus winning it for the first time in the county's history. They played 22 matches during the season with 16 wins, 3 defeats and 4 draws. On the way to the Championship, Kent notched up a record twelve successive wins. This picture was taken in advance of Kent recording a total of 610 versus Hampshire at Bournemouth. It was also in this season that Kent recorded 471 against the West Indians at Canterbury.

James Seymour was born in West Hoathly in 1879. He represented the county between 1902 and 1926 and in his 536 matches he recorded 26,818 runs (av. 32.62) and amassed 53 hundreds. His highest innings was 218 not out versus Essex at the County Ground, Leyton, in 1911. He took 15 wickets (av. 45.33) with a best performance of 4 for 62 and held 659 catches. His benefit match in 1920 against Hampshire ended up as a test court case that went to the House of Lords, the final decision being that cricketers' benefit match proceeds would not be taxable. He died at Marden in 1930.

Kent fielding at Canterbury in 1906 from the painting by Albert Chevallier Tayler. The participants are, from left to right: E. Humphreys (mid-on), E.W. Dillon (in front of screen), W. Findlay (batsman at bowler's end), A.J. Atfield (umpire), C. Blythe (bowler), J.T. Tyldesley (batting), R.N.R. Blaker (mid-off), F.H. Huish (wicketkeeper), K.L. Hutchings (on boundary), C.H.B. Marsham (extra-cover), A. Fielder (point), J.R. Mason (slip), C.J. Burnup (cover) and J. Seymour (third-man).

Captain of Oxford University in 1902 and Kent between 1904 and 1908, Henry Marsham was born in Bicester in 1879. Playing his early cricket at Eton and Oxford University, he attained blues in 1900, 1901 and 1902 and represented Kent between 1900 and 1922 in 141 matches. A sound middle-order batsman, he scored 4,397 runs (av. 20.93) with a highest innings of 128 versus Essex at Tonbridge in 1908 and held 74 catches. His best season was 1904 when he amassed 1,070 runs (av. 28.91). He later played Minor County cricket for Shropshire and was a Test selector in 1907. He died at Wrotham Hill, Kent, in 1928.

Representing Kent between 1899 and 1920, E. Humphreys played 366 matches for the county, scoring 15,308 runs (av. 28.03) and taking 306 wickets (av. 26.54). He held 212 catches during his career.

Kent CCC, 1907. From left to right, back row: W. Hearne (scorer), A. Fielder, K.L. Hutchings, F.H. Huish, C. Blythe. Middle row: R.N.R. Blaker, J.R. Mason, C.H.B. Marsham (captain), E.W. Dillon, C.J. Burnup. Front row: J. Seymour, H.T.W. Hardinge, W.J. Fairservice, F.E. Woolley, E. Humphreys. Kent finished in eighth place in the County Championship, with 12 wins, 9 defeats and 5 draws.

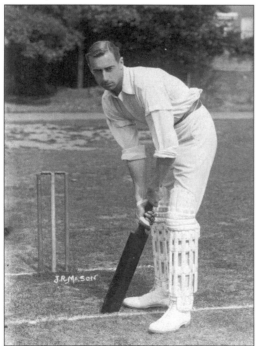

Born in Blackheath in 1874, John Mason represented Kent between 1893 and 1914 in 300 matches, during which time he accumulated 15,563 runs (av. 33.98) with 31 hundreds and a top score of 183 versus Somerset at Blackheath in 1897. He amassed 769 wickets (av. 22.06) with a best bowling performance of 8 for 29 versus Somerset at Taunton in 1901 and he held 360 catches. He captained the county between 1898 and 1902 and acted as president in 1939. He died at Cooden Beach in 1958.

Born in 1881 at Penge, Edward Dillon learnt his early cricket while at Rugby School and Oxford University, where he attained Blues in 1901 and 1902. A hard-hitting left-handed batsman and useful leg-break bowler, he made his debut for Kent in 1900. During the same season he also represented the London County Club at Crystal Palace, scoring 108 on his debut for the side led and organised by W.G. Grace against Worcestershire. A notable rugby footballer, he played three-quarter for both Blackheath and England during his career with the oval ball. He played 223 matches for Kent before his retirement from the game in 1923. Dillon scored 9,415 runs (av. 28.88) with a top score of 141, bagged 27 wickets (av. 48.92) with a best performance of 3 for 20 and held 195 catches. He toured the West Indies with Bennett's side in 1901/02 and went to North America with Kent in 1903. He died in Totteridge, Hertfordshire, in 1941.

K.L. Hutchings (Kent), C.H.B. Marsham (Kent) and W.G. Grace at Canterbury in 1908.

Kent CCC, 1908. From left to right, back row: C. Blythe, F.E. Woolley, J. Seymour, W. Hearne (scorer), W.J. Fairservice, E. Humphreys, A. Fielder. Front row: H.T.W. Hardinge, E.W. Dillon, C.H.B. Marsham (captain), K.L. Hutchings, F.H. Huish. Kent finished in second place in the County Championship; 25 matches were played with 17 wins, 3 defeats and 5 draws. Kent recorded their highest innings totals against three counties during the season: 615 versus Derbyshire at Derby, 561 versus Northamptonshire at Gravesend and 601 for 8 declared versus Somerset at Taunton. The lattermost game included four hundreds in an innings for the first time for the county – J. Seymour (129), F.E. Woolley (105), A.P. Day (118) and E. Humphreys (149) all recorded centuries.

Colin Blythe made his debut for Kent in 1899 versus Yorkshire at Tonbridge and he bowled Frank Mitchell with his first delivery. In the fourteen seasons that followed he only once failed to take 100 wickets in a season. 'Charlie' Blythe was a slow left-arm bowler and one of the most outstanding bowlers of the golden age of Kent cricket. He played 381 matches for Kent, taking 2,210 wickets (av. 16.67) and scoring 3,964 runs (av. 10.03) with a top score of 82 not out. He took ten wickets in a match on 64 occasions and held 183 catches. In 1907 he achieved the remarkable feat of taking 10 for 30 in an innings and 17 for 48 in the match, all in one day versus Northamptonshire at Wantage Road, Northampton. A nervous performer, he played 19 Tests, taking 100 wickets (av. 18.63) with a best performance of 8 for 59 versus South Africa at Headingley in 1907, and he scored 183 runs (av. 9.63) with a highest score of 27 versus South Africa at Cape Town in 1905/06. He toured abroad four times and was a good violinist who also enjoyed watching a bout of boxing from time to time. In 1917, while serving as a sergeant in the Kent Fortress Engineers, he was killed on the Western Front and a memorial to him stands at the St Lawrence Cricket Ground.

William Fairservice was born in Nunhead in 1881. The father of Colin, who represented Kent between 1929 and 1933, he was a right-arm, medium-pace bowler who occasionally bowled off-breaks and was a right-handed, tail-end batsman. He bagged 853 wickets (av. 22.59) with a best haul of 7 for 44, held 164 catches and scored 4,922 runs (av. 15.33) with a top score for the county of 61 not out. His best season was 1920 when he took 113 wickets (av. 17.46). After retiring from first-class cricket he played three seasons of minor county cricket for Northumberland between 1924 and 1926. He died in Canterbury in 1971.

Kent CCC, pictured during the Tunbridge Wells Cricket Week, 1908. From left to right, back row: C. Blythe, F.E. Woolley, W. Hearne (scorer), A. Fielder, E. Humphreys, W.J. Fairservice. Front row: F.W. Huish, H.T.W. Hardinge, C.J. Burnup, C.H.B. Marsham (captain), K.L. Hutchings, J. Seymour. Two matches were scheduled at the Nevill Ground during the

cricket festival. They were against Lancashire on 13, 14 and 15 July and against Middlesex on 16, 17 and 18 July 1908. The match with Lancashire was not completed due to rain: Kent scored 76 and 65 for 3 with Lancashire replying with 130. The following game against Middlesex was abandoned without a ball being bowled.

George Collins was a lower-order, left-handed batsman and right-arm, fast-medium bowler. Born in Gravesend in 1889, he represented his native county from 1911 to 1928 in 212 matches. During his career he scored 6,237 runs (av. 22.35) with a top score of 110 versus Leicestershire at Leicester in 1926, took 378 wickets (av. 23.71) with a best of 10 for 65 versus Nottinghamshire at Dover in 1922 and held 79 catches (also managing a single stumping). He died at Rochester, Kent, in 1949.

Kent CCC, 1909. From left to right, back row: F.E. Woolley, J.R. Mason, E. Humphreys, W. Hearne (scorer), W.J. Fairservice, S.H. Day, J. Seymour, A.P. Day, H.T.W. Hardinge. Front row: A. Fielder, K.L. Hutchings, E.W. Dillon (captain), F.W. Huish, C. Blythe. Kent finished as county champions, winning the competition for the second time. Of the 26 matches played during the season they won 16, lost 2 and drew 8 of them. Colin Blythe recorded 9 for 42 in an innings and 16 for 102 in the match against Leicestershire at Leicester.

F.E. Woolley (185) and A. Fielder (112) in front of the scoreboard at Stourbridge on 7 July 1909 after the two had added a record 235 for the tenth wicket for Kent against Worcestershire, the home side.

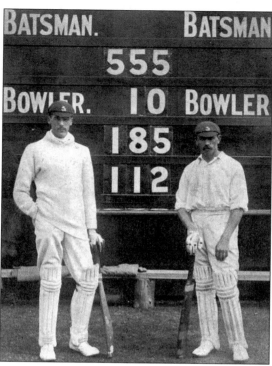

Born at Southborough in 1882, a true man of Kent, Kenneth Hutchings hit 205 while still at Tonbridge School. He made his debut for the county at nineteen years of age in 1902 and recorded the first of his 19 centuries against Somerset at Taunton in 1903. His best season was 1906, when Kent secured their first County Championship, during which he amassed 1,454 runs (av. 60.68) including his highest score of 176 versus Lancashire at Canterbury (made in just three hours). He toured abroad with A.O. Jones' team to Australia in 1907/08 and scored 126 (106 in boundaries) at Melbourne. A forceful right-handed batsman, he had particularly strong wrists and forearms which assisted his stroke-play and when fielding on the boundary. He played 163 matches for Kent, scoring 7,977 runs (av. 35.29) and exceeded 1,000 runs in a season six times. He also claimed 15 wickets (av. 32.86) and held 141 catches. Hutchings represented England in 7 Tests, scoring 341 runs (av. 28.41). A Lieutenant in the 4th Battalion of the King's Liverpool Regiment, he was killed during the First World War.

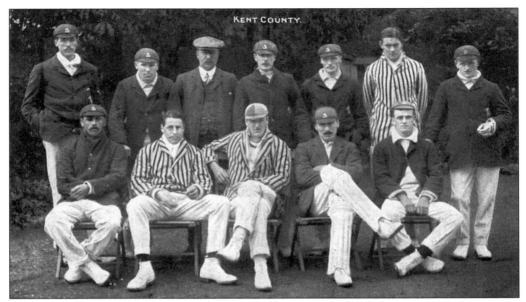

Kent CCC, 1910. From left to right, back row: F.E. Woolley, E. Humphreys, W. Hearne (scorer), W.J. Fairservice, J. Seymour, A.P. Day, H.T.W. Hardinge. Front row: A. Fielder, K.L. Hutchings, E.W. Dillon (captain), F.H. Huish, C. Blythe. Kent again finished in first place in the County Championship, winning it for the third time and the second year in succession. They recorded 16 wins, 2 defeats and 8 draws. While playing Gloucestershire at Cheltenham College, Kent amassed a record 607 for 6 declared against the West Country county.

Arthur Fielder was a right-arm fast bowler and late-order right-handed batsman who represented Kent between 1900 and 1914 in 253 matches. Born at Plaxtol near Tonbridge in 1877, his most famous performance was when he took ten wickets in an innings at Lord's for just 90 runs while representing the Players versus the Gentlemen in 1906. During his county career he bagged 1,150 wickets (av. 20.88) with a best haul of 9 for 108 versus Lancashire at Canterbury in 1907. He also scored 2,000 runs (av. 11.42) with a top score of 112 not out versus Worcestershire at Stourbridge in 1909 when he came to the wicket at no. 11. He held a total of 106 catches during his career. Fielder played 6 Tests for England between 1903/04 and 1907/08, touring Australia twice. He died in Lambeth in 1949.

Kent CCC, 1911. From left to right, back row: E. Humphreys, W.J. Fairservice, D.W. Jennings, F.E. Woolley, C. Blythe, J. Seymour, H.T.W. Hardinge. Front row: F.H. Huish, A.P. Day, K.L. Hutchings (captain), S.H. Day, A. Fielder. Kent finished in second place in the County Championship with 17 wins, 4 defeats and 5 draws. At the Northlands Road ground in Southampton, Kent set Hampshire, the home side, a mammoth fourth innings total of 568 to win. Hampshire ended on 493 for 8.

Kent CCC, 1913. From left to right, back row: W. Hearne (scorer), C. Blythe, E. Humphreys, J. Seymour, J.C. Hubble, W.J. Fairservice. Middle row: F.E. Woolley, C.E. Hatfield, E.W. Dillon (captain), W.A. Powell, F.H. Huish. Front row: H.T.W. Hardinge, D.W. Jennings. This side won the County Championship for the fourth time in the county's history, with 20 wins, 3 defeats and 5 draws. Kent dismissed Warwickshire for just 16 at Tonbridge in the course of a season which also saw Frank Woolley record the highest individual innings for the county, against Oxford University, with 224 not out at the University Parks.

Born in Greenwich in 1886, Harold Hardinge was a noted double international who represented England at both soccer and cricket (although for only a single Test in 1921). A right-handed top-order batsman and slow left-arm bowler, he represented Kent between 1902 and 1933, during which time he played 606 matches. He amassed 32,549 runs (av. 36.48) with 73 centuries and a top score of 263 not out versus Gloucestershire at Gloucester in 1928. He also bagged 370 wickets (av. 26.41) with a best haul of 5 for 31 and held 286 catches. He hit 1,000 runs in a season eighteen times and over 2,000 runs five times, with a best aggregate of 2,446 runs (av. 59.65) in 1928. Capped by England in 1910 at soccer, he played inside-left, representing Newcastle United, Sheffield United and Arsenal. After retiring from the game he worked for the John Wisden and Company sports firm. Hardinge died in Cambridge in 1965.

Kent CCC, 1914. From left to right, back row: A. Fielder, J. Seymour, J.C. Hubble, W. Hearne (captain), F.E. Woolley, D.W. Jennings, A.P. Freeman, W.J. Fairservice. Front row: F.H. Huish, A.P. Day, L.H.W. Troughton (captain), H.T.W. Hardinge, C. Blythe. Kent finished in third place in the County Championship with 16 wins, 7 defeats and 5 draws. The county recorded its highest innings total against Yorkshire during the season with 493 at Tonbridge. The prolific Frank Woolley achieved the coveted season double of 2,192 runs and 119 wickets.

A wooden plaque erected at the St Lawrence Cricket Ground in memory of A.P. 'Tich' Freeman.

Alfred Percy 'Tich' Freeman, surely the greatest wicket-taker county cricket has ever known, was only 5ft 2ins tall. Born in Lewisham in 1888, he joined Kent at Tonbridge in 1912 and made his debut versus Oxford University at the University Parks in 1914. A right-arm, leg-spin bowler, he had a particularly good top-spinner, which many opposing batsmen found difficult to spot. In 1922 'Tich' took 194 wickets and was rewarded with a place on the MCC tour to Australia and New Zealand, making his maiden fifty in first-class cricket during his first Test match at Sydney. His most successful summer was 1928, when he became the first bowler to take 300 wickets in a season. Tich took 100 wickets in a month in 1930 and became the first bowler to take all ten wickets three times in first-class cricket. Playing 506 matches for Kent, he captured 3,340 wickets (av. 17.64) with a best performance of 10 for 53, scored 4,257 runs (av. 9.25) and held 202 catches. He played 12 Tests, taking 66 wickets (av. 25.86) with a best return of 7 for 71 versus South Africa at Old Trafford in 1928. After retiring he played for Walsall CC in the Birmingham League.

Kent CCC, 1919. From left to right, back row: W.J. Fairservice, G. C. Collins, W. Hearne (scorer), J. Seymour, J.C. Hubble, A.P. Freeman. Front row: H.T.W. Hardinge, A.P. Hedges,

L.H.W. Troughton (captain), Captain W.S. Cornwallis, A.F. Bickmore, F.E. Woolley. Kent finished as runners-up in the County Championship with 6 wins, 1 defeat and 7 draws.

Making his Kent debut versus Lancashire at Old Trafford in 1906, Frank Woolley played a record 764 matches for the county, scoring 47,868 runs (av. 41.77) with 122 centuries and a top score of 270 versus Middlesex at Canterbury in 1933. With a height of 6ft and 3in, he was the finest and most elegant all-rounder to have represented Kent, taking 1,680 wickets (av. 18.84) with a best performance of 8 for 22 and holding 773 catches. He made the first of his 64 Test appearances versus Australia at Kennington Oval in 1909 (the season he added 235 for the tenth wicket versus Worcestershire at Stourbridge with Arthur Fielder). He scored 3,283 Test runs (av. 36.07) with 5 centuries and his top score was 154 versus South Africa at Old Trafford in 1929. Touring abroad seven times, he took 83 wickets (av. 33.91) with a best performance of 7 for 76 versus New Zealand at Wellington in 1929/30 and held 64 catches. Having scored 2,894 runs (av. 59.06) in 1928, it was surprising that he had been turned down for Army duty during the First World War on grounds of poor eyesight. After retiring he coached guests at Butlin's holiday camp in Clacton-on-Sea before moving to reside in Canada, where he died in 1978.

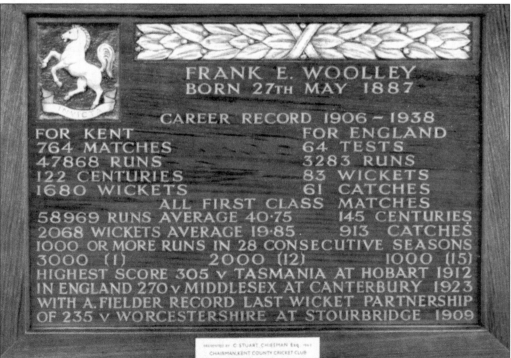

A wooden plaque erected at the St Lawrence Cricket Ground in memory of Frank E. Woolley, the greatest of Kent batsman.

Three
Woolley, Chapman, Ames and the Folkestone Festival

Kent CCC, 1920. From left to right, back row: W. Hearne (scorer), A.P. Freeman, W. Ashdown, H.T.W. Hardinge, C. Wright, F.E. Woolley, C.S. Hurst, G.C. Collins, J.C. Hubble. Front row: G.J. Bryan, A.F. Bickmore, L.H.W. Troughton (captain), Capt. W.S. Cornwallis, C.J. Capes. Kent finished in fifth place in the County Championship with 16 wins, 6 defeats and 4 draws. Frank Woolley again achieved the coveted seasonal double of 1,548 runs and 164 wickets.

E.W. Dillon, J.R. Mason and R.N.R. Blaker.

Born in Borstal in 1895, Charles Wright was a hard-hitting, lower-order, right-handed batsman and right-arm medium-fast bowler who represented Kent in 225 matches from 1921 to 1931. He took 596 wickets (av. 24.26) with a best performance of 7 for 31, held 127 catches and scored 3,280 runs (av. 13.09) with a highest innings of 81. His best season was 1927 when he bagged 107 wickets (av. 20.38). He died in Westminster, London, in 1959.

Kent CCC, 1921. From left to right, back row: G.C. Collins, W.J. Fairservice, F.E. Woolley, J.C. Hubble, H.T.W. Hardinge. Front row: J. Seymour, A.P. Hedges, Captain W.S. Cornwallis, L.H.W. Troughton (captain), A.F. Bickmore, A.P. Freeman. Kent finished in fourth place in the County Championship with 16 wins, 7 defeats and 3 draws. The Australians visited the St Lawrence Ground and their batsman flayed the Kent bowling to such an extent that the touring batsmen recorded 676, their highest innings total against the county.

Kent CCC, 1922. From left to right, back row: H.T.W. Hardinge, A.P. Freeman, J.C. Hubble, G.C. Collins, J. Seymour, W.H. Ashdown. Front row: C.J. Capes, A.J. Evans, L.H.W. Troughton (captain), A.F. Bickmore, F.E. Woolley. Kent finished fourth in the County Championship with 16 wins, 3 defeats and 9 draws. H.T.W. Hardinge recorded the highest individual innings for Kent of 249 not out against Leicestershire at Leicester and two individual performances with the ball were worthy of note: Tich Freeman took 9 for 11 in an innings and match figures of 17 for 67 versus Sussex at Hove and G.C. Collins took 10 for 65 in an innings and match figures of 16 for 83 versus Nottinghamshire at Dover.

Born in Bromley in 1898, Bill Ashdown represented Kent between 1920 and 1937, during which time he played 482 matches and hit 22,309 runs (av. 30.64) with 38 centuries. His highest individual innings was a massive 332 against Essex at Brentwood in 1934. Bill also bagged 595 wickets (av. 32.42), with a best haul of 6 for 23, and held 398 catches (as well as a stumping). He later coached Leicestershire between 1951 and 1961, moving to become scorer between 1966 to 1969. He died at Rugby in 1979.

Kent CCC, 1923. From left to right, back row: G.C. Collins, J.C. Hubble, J. Seymour, W. Hearne (scorer), H.T.W. Hardinge, W. Ashdown, F.E. Woolley. Front row: A.P. Freeman, C.S. Hurst, L.H.W. Troughton (captain), L.P. Hedges, C.J. Bryan. Kent finished fifth in the County Championship with 16 wins, 8 defeats and 4 draws. Jack Hubble, the Kent wicketkeeper, took the most dismissals in a match for the county with 10 (9 catches and a stumping) against Gloucestershire at Cheltenham.

Action from the Kent versus Middlesex County Championship match during the Canterbury Cricket Week of 1923.

Kent CCC, 1925. Kent finished in fifth place in the County Championship with 15 wins, 7 defeats and 6 draws. From left to right, back row: A. Hearne (scorer), C. Wright, J. Seymour, L.J. Todd, H.T.W. Hardinge, W. Ashdown. Front row: F.E. Woolley, A.P.F. Chapman, Capt. W.S. Cornwallis (captain), G.B. Legge, A.P. Freeman.

Born in Reading, Percy Chapman was an adventurous left-handed batsman and fine gully fielder. He topped the batting average (with 111.33) at Uppingham School in 1917 and scored 118 for Cambridge University versus Essex at Fenner's on his first-class debut in 1920, achieving a Blue as a freshman. Prior to joining Kent in 1924, he represented his native Berkshire and played for England while still active in Minor County cricket. He captained England in 17 of his 26 Tests, winning a record first nine games and regaining the Ashes at Kennington Oval in 1926. He scored 925 runs (av. 28.90) with a top score of 121 versus Australia at Lord's in 1930 and became the only batsman to score centuries at Lord's against Australia, for the Gentlemen versus the Players and in a University Varsity game. He held 32 catches and toured abroad three times. A popular, friendly person he captained Kent from 1931 to 1936, making 194 appearances for the county and scoring 6,681 runs (av. 26.93) with 8 centuries. His highest score of 260 versus Lancashire at Maidstone in 1927 is the highest individual innings on the ground for Kent in a first-class match.

Conrad Powell Johnstone was born in Sydenham in 1895 and represented Kent in 36 matches between 1919 and 1933. A left-handed opening batsman he accumulated 1,186 runs (av. 21.96) with a top score of 102 against Gloucestershire at Maidstone in 1925. He also took 8 wickets (av. 25.50) with a best of 3 for 4 with his right-arm medium-pace bowling and held 18 catches. Schooled at Rugby and Cambridge University, he attained Blues in both 1919 and 1920. He represented the Europeans from 1926/27 to 1947/48 and Madras between 1934/35 and 1944/45 while serving in India. He was awarded the CBE for his services to the game of cricket in Madras and also served Kent as president in 1966. He died at Eastry (near Sandwich) in 1974.

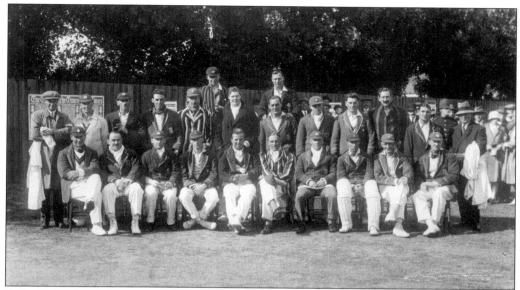

Folkestone Cricket Festival team groups, comprised of A.E.R. Gilligan's XI and their opponents, Hon. L.H. Tennyson's XI. The contest was staged at the Cheriton Road ground on 9, 10 and 11 September 1925. The high-scoring match lasted only two innings and ended in a draw, with Hon. L.H. Tennyson's XI amassing 415 for 6 innings closed (E.H. Bowley 120, W.R. Hammond 120, C.P. Mead 88) and A.E.R. Gilligan's XI 384 (A. Sandham 69, J.B. Hobbs 64, M.W. Tate 55, H.A. Peach 53, J.L. Bryan 45, C.W.L. Parker 6 for 101).

Colchester Cricket Festival – 2, 3 and 4 June 1926. The teams were Kent and Essex and the match was staged at Colchester Garrison 'A' Ground. Essex scored 108 (J.A. Cutmore 55, A.P. Freeman 5 for 25, A.C. Wright 4 for 29) and 172 (M.S. Nichols 49, H.M. Morris 41, A.P. Freeman 5 for 60) and Kent scored 146 (A.P. Freeman 45, J.A. Deed 37, M.S. Nichols 6 for 61) and 132 for 8 (J. Seymour 39, M.S. Nichols 4 for 65, L.C. Eastman 4 for 49). Although the match was drawn, it will be remembered as Freeman of Kent's match.

Hon. L.H. Tennyson's XI pictured at the Cheriton Road ground during Folkestone Cricket Festival, September 1926. The team included, in batting order: G. Brown, R.E.S. Wyatt, F.E. Woolley, W.H. Ashdown, Revd F.H. Gillingham, Hon. L.H. Tennyson, G.E. Livock, A.H.H. Gilligan, A.P. Freeman, H. Larwood, J.J. Thorley.

Calthorpe's XI pictured at the Cheriton Road ground during Folkestone Cricket Festival, September 1926. The team included, in batting order: H.L. Dales, J. Newman, E.J. Smith, E.H. Hendren, C.H. Knott, Hon. F.S.G. Calthorpe, W.E. Astill, G.W. Stephens, F. Root, G.M. Louden, T.J. Durston.

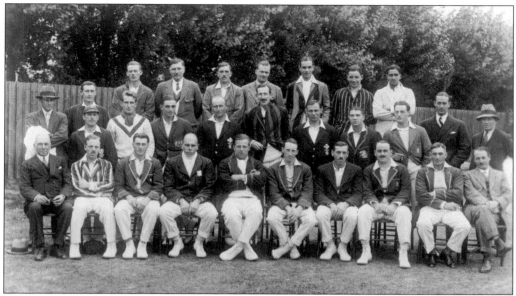

Folkestone Cricket Festival joint teams comprising Hon. L.H. Tennyson's XI and Hon. F.S.G. Calthorpe's XI. The game was staged at the Cheriton Road ground in Folkestone on 4, 6 and 7 September 1926. Hon. L.H. Tennyson's XI scored 386 (A.H.H. Gilligan 94, Revd F.H. Gillingham 72, F.J. Durston 4 for 98) and 179 for 6 innings closed (G. Brown 71), while Hon. F.S.G. Calthorpe's XI managed 311 (J. Newman 79, H.L. Dales 49, H. Larwood 6 for 109) and 100 for 1 (H.L. Dales 57 not out). This second match of the Folkestone Festival resulted in a draw.

England XI versus the touring Australians at the Cheriton Road ground during Folkestone Cricket Festival, September 1926. The team included, in batting order: R.E.S. Wyatt, D.R. Jardine, F.E. Woolley, E.H. Hendren, Hon. F.S.G. Calthorpe, A.P.F. Chapman, Hon. L.H. Tennyson, W.E. Astill, E.J. Smith, A.P. Freeman, H. Larwood.

My Sports House

offers you a selection of all that is best in the world of sport and comprises:—

CRICKET
TENNIS
FOOTBALL
BADMINTON
HOCKEY
BILLIARDS
Etc., Etc.

TENNIS COURTS
completely
furnished.

CLUBS of all kinds
specially catered for

CATALOGUES
in due seasons.

Enquiries Invited.

JACK HUBBLE,
THE KENTISH SPORTS HOUSE,
MAIDSTONE.

Advertisement for Jack Hubble's Kentish Sports House at Maidstone, 1923. Hubble scored 10,229 runs (av. 23.51) with 5 centuries for Kent, including a highest individual innings of 189. He also took 411 catches and 217 stumpings during his county career, which spanned 343 matches between 1904 and 1929.

Kent CCC, 1926. From left to right, back row: G.C. Collins, J.C. Hubble, C. Wright, F.E. Woolley, W. Ashdown, A.P. Freeman. Front row: H.T.W. Hardinge, F.E. Woolley, Captain W.S. Cornwallis (captain), G.B. Legge, J. Seymour. Kent finished third in the County Championship with 15 wins, 2 defeats and 11 draws. At the County Ground, Northampton, Frank Woolley recorded the highest individual innings for the county against Northamptonshire with 217.

The Hon. L.H. Tennyson during the wreath-laying ceremony at the Colin Blythe Memorial, St Lawrence Cricket Ground, Canterbury, 1926. This ceremony continues today and is carried out annually by members of the Kent County Cricket Club and members of the Kent County Cricket Club Supporters' Club in August.

Kent CCC, 1927. From left to right, back row: J.C. Hubble, W. Ashdown, G.C. Collins, C. Wright, C.J. Capes, L.E.G. Ames, A.P. Freeman, W. Hearne (scorer). Front row: H.T.W. Hardinge, A.P.F. Chapman, A.J. Evans (captain), G.B. Legge, F.E. Woolley. Kent finished fourth in the County Championship with 12 wins, 6 defeats and 10 draws. Frank Woolley recorded the highest seasonal batting average by a Kent player of 70.35 from 15 innings.

Born in Catford in 1907, Leslie Todd was a left-handed batsman and left-arm bowler who represented the county from 1927 to 1950 in 426 matches. Achieving the coveted double in 1947 with 2,312 runs and 103 wickets, he was also a useful amateur soccer player with Dulwich Hamlet and played table tennis for England. He scored 19,407 runs (av. 31.50) with 36 centuries, of which his highest score was 174 versus Leicestershire at Maidstone in 1949. He took a total of 555 wickets (av. 27.38), with a best performance of 6 for 26, and held 226 catches. He died in Dover in 1967.

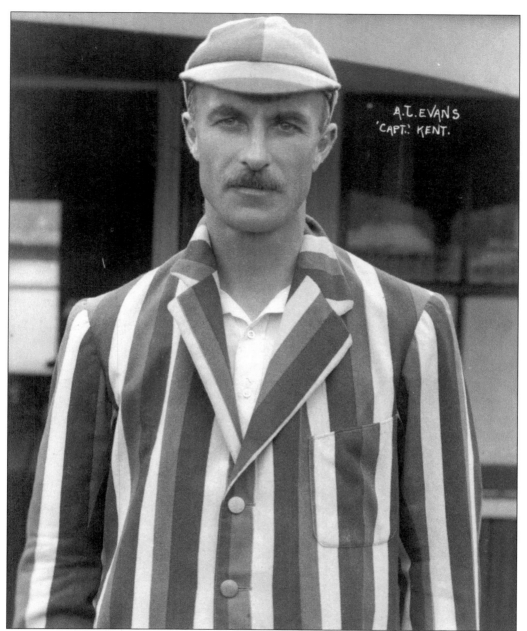

Alfred Evans was born in Newtown, Hampshire, in 1899 and represented Kent between 1921 and 1928 in 36 matches. A right-handed batsman and bowler, he scored 1,303 runs (av. 25.05) with a top score of 143 versus Lancashire at Maidstone in 1927. He also took 19 wickets (av. 31.84) and held 41 catches. He nephew, brother and cousin all played for Hampshire, where he originally commenced his career (although he only played 7 matches for his native county between 1908 and 1920). Alfred attained blues in every year while at Oxford University between 1909 and 1912 and played a single Test for England in 1921. He captained Oxford University in 1911 and Kent in 1927. During the First World War he became famous for his escapes from German POW camps.

Kent CCC, 1928. From left to right, back row: A.P. Freeman, L.E.G. Ames, C. Wright, G.C. Collins, C.J. Capes, W.H. Ashdown. Front row: F.E. Woolley, A.P.F. Chapman, Captain W.S. Cornwallis (captain), L.B. Legge, H.T.W. Hardinge. Kent finished as runners-up in the County Championship with 15 wins, 5 defeats and 10 draws. Three significant performances included Tich Freeman's 9 for 104 in an innings (with match figures of 11 for 191) against the touring West Indians at Canterbury, Frank Woolley's 2,894 runs for the county during the season and Kent's record innings total against Middlesex at Lord's of 539 for 9 declared.

Kent CCC, 1929. From left to right, back row: W.H. Ashdown, H.T.W. Hardinge, J. Seymour, G.C. Collins, F.E. Woolley, C. Wright, A.E. Watt. Middle row: A.M. Crawley, J.C. Hubble, G.B. Legge (captain), G.J. Capes. Front row: A.P. Freeman. Kent finished eighth in the County Championship with 12 wins, 8 defeats and 8 draws. Les Ames recorded a season double of 1,777 runs and 116 dismissals (71 catches and 45 stumpings) and Kent scored a record 513 for 9 declared against MCC at Lord's.

Kent CCC, 1931. From left to right, back row: W.H. Ashdown, L.E.G. Ames, C. Wright, A.E. Watt, T.C. Longfield, A.M. Crawley. Front row: H.T.W. Hardinge, B.H. Valentine, A.P.F. Chapman (captain), F.E. Woolley, A.P. Freeman. Kent finished third in the County Championship with 12 wins, 7 defeats and 9 draws. They recorded their highest innings total of 437 versus the touring New Zealanders at Canterbury, which included 224 from the bat of Frank Woolley (who added 227 for the fifth wicket with Les Ames). Other outstanding performances included Tich Freeman's 8 for 99 in an innings with match figures of 13 for 184 against Oxford University at the University Parks and C.S. Marriott's 7 for 58 in an innings with match figures of 12 for 160 against the New Zealanders at Canterbury. Frank Woolley recorded 188, the highest individual innings for Kent against Yorkshire, at Bradford's Park Avenue ground.

A.P.F. Chapman leads out his Kent side to field at the Nevill Cricket Ground, Tunbridge Wells, in 1932.

Associated with Kent for sixty-six years until his death in 1990, Les Ames was a right-handed opening batsman and wicketkeeper. He played 430 matches for the county, scoring 29,851 runs (av. 44.33) with 78 centuries and a top score of 295 against Gloucestershire at Folkestone in 1933. He took 512 catches and 330 stumpings and even bowled as well, taking 22 wickets (av. 31.68). In 1929 he set a wicketkeeping record of 127 dismissals in a season and made his Test debut versus South Africa at Kennington Oval. Making five tours abroad, he played 47 Tests for England, scoring 2,434 runs (av. 40.56) with 8 centuries of which his highest score was 149 versus West Indies at Sabina Park in 1929/30. He managed a total of 97 dismissals for his country. Ames scored his 100th century versus Middlesex at the St Lawrence Ground in 1950 and became the first wicketkeeper to accomplish this feat. An England selector from 1950 to 1958, he acted as MCC tour manager abroad and was manager of Kent from 1957 to 1974. In 1975 he became only the second professional after Frank Woolley to be elected a member of the Band of Brothers and was awarded the CBE for his services to cricket.

Kent CCC, 1932. From left to right: H.T.W. Hardinge, T.A. Pearce, A.P. Freeman, A.E, Watt, C.S. Marriott, B.H. Valentine, A.P.F. Chapman (captain), W.H. Ashdown, L.E.G. Ames, A.M. Crawley, F.E. Woolley. Kent finished third in the County Championship with 14 wins, 3 defeats and 10 draws. Tich Freeman achieved two outstanding performances with 9 for 61 in an innings (match figures of 17 for 92) against Warwickshire at Folkestone and 6 for 69 in an innings (match figures of 9 for 155) versus the Indians at Canterbury.

LESLIE E. G. AMES
BORN 3RD DECEMBER 1905

CAREER RECORD
37245 RUNS   HIGHEST SCORE 295 (v. GLOUCS)
102 CENTURIES   AVERAGE 43·56
1000 RUNS IN SEASON (17 TIMES) 2000 (5 TIMES) 3000 (ONCE)
IN 1933 57 INNINGS   3058 RUNS   AVERAGE 58·80
TWO SEPARATE HUNDREDS IN A MATCH 3 TIMES
THE LAWRENCE TROPHY (FASTEST 100) 1936 AND 1939
415 STUMPINGS (A RECORD) AND 688 CAUGHT
121 WICKETS IN 1928 & 127 WICKETS IN 1929 (A RECORD)
IN 1932 2482 RUNS AND 100 WICKETS (A RECORD)
FOR ENGLAND
47 TESTS 2434 RUNS 8 CENTURIES AVERAGE 40·56
TEST SELECTOR 1950-1956 AND 1958
APPTD SEC./MANAGER KENT C.C.C. 1960

A wooden plaque erected at the St Lawrence Cricket Ground in memory of Leslie E.G. Ames, the greatest of Kent wicketkeepers.

Kent CCC in 1932, as depicted on a Barratt & Company trade card. From left to right, back row: C. Fairservice, A.E. Watt, A.M. Crawley, L.E.G. Ames, H.T.W. Hardinge, B.H. Valentine. Front row: W.H. Ashdown, A.P.F. Chapman, L.J. Todd, A. Blunden, F.E. Woolley, A.P. Freeman.

A most gifted all-round athlete, Bryan Valentine excelled at lawn tennis while studying at Repton School and later at Cambridge University, where he also collected Blues at cricket and was a useful golfer. He made his debut for Kent in 1927, although he did not secure a regular place in the county side until 1931. In 1933 he scored 1,653 runs (av. 36.73) and was chosen for the MCC tour of India in 1933/34. He hit 134 versus India at Bombay on his Test debut and went on to play in a total of 7 Tests, scoring 454 runs (av. 64.85) with two centuries. At Oakham in 1938 versus Leicestershire he made his highest score of 242 and in 1938/39 he toured South Africa, scoring 112 at Cape Town. He was awarded the MC during the Second World War and captained Kent from 1946 to 1948. He made 308 appearances for the county, scoring 14,131 runs (av. 30.52) with 25 centuries and taking 243 catches. He became club president in 1967 and served on the club committee for many years until his death in 1983.

Hopper Levett was born in Gouldhurst in 1908 and he played 142 matches for the county between 1930 and 1947. He scored 2,054 runs (av. 12.08) with a top score of 76. A competent wicketkeeper, he took 228 catches and 169 stumpings. Hopper played for England once in India and Ceylon in 1933/34 and acted as president of the county club in 1974.

Kent CCC, 1933. From left to right, back row: C.C. Lewis, W.H. Ashdown, A.E. Watt, W.H.V. Levett, J.D.W. Davies, A.E. Fagg, L.J. Todd. Front row: F.E. Woolley, I.S. Akers-Douglas, A.P.F. Chapman (captain), B.H. Valentine, A.P. Freeman. Kent finished third in the County Championship with 15 wins, 8 defeats and 7 draws. Significant individual batting performances for the county included 210 by Les Ames versus Warwickshire at Tonbridge and 154 not out by C. H. Knott versus the West Indians at Canterbury. With the ball, Tich Freeman achieved a record 262 wickets in a season for the county.

Kent CCC, 1934. This team group includes: J. Seymour, C. Wright, F.E. Woolley, H.T.W. Hardinge, W.H. Ashdown, W.H.V. Levett, A.P.F. Chapman, J.C. Hubble, A.P. Freeman. Kent finished in fifth place in the County Championship. Of their 30 matches, they won 12 and lost 7 with 11 draws. During this season Kent recorded their highest innings total in the history of the club with 803 for 4 declared versus Essex at Brentwood.

From left to right: L.E.G. Ames, A.P.F. Chapman and A.P. Freeman pictured in blazers at Tonbridge in 1934.

Three of the men responsible for the mammoth 803 for 4 declared total against Essex at Brentwood on 31 May 1934. From left to right: W.H. Ashdown (332), L.E.G. Ames (202 not out) and F.E. Woolley (172).

Kent CCC, 1935. The team group includes: I.S. Akers-Douglas, W.H. Ashdown, L.E.G. Ames, W.H.V. Levett, B.H. Valentine, A.P.F. Chapman (captain), H.T.W. Hardinge, A.P. Freeman. Kent finished tenth in the County Championship with 10 wins, 12 defeats and 7 draws. Kent recorded their highest innings total against Surrey at The Oval with 579 for 8 declared, with Frank Woolley hitting 229 runs. Also during the season, Bill Ashdown hit 305 not out at the Crabble Athletic Ground against Derbyshire and Kent were dismissed by Leicestershire at Oakham School for just 56.

Standing left to right:
A.P.F. Chapman, A.P. Freeman and F.E. Woolley, pictured in blazers at Dover in 1935.

Kent CCC, 1936. Kent finished in eighth place in the County Championship with 9 wins, 9 defeats and 10 draws. Three county records were broken during the tour match with the Indians at the St Lawrence Ground during the season. The Kent innings total of 523 was their highest against India and included Arthur Fagg's record score of 172, which in turn was part of a record first wicket stand of 221 put on with Bill Ashdown.

Standing left to right at the St Lawrence ground in 1956: A.P. Freeman (Kent), A.P.F. Chapman (Kent) and Nawab of Pataudi (Sussex).

Kent CCC, 1937. The side included: A.P. Freeman, L.E.G. Ames, C. Wright, W.H. Ashdown, F.E. Woolley, A.P.F. Chapman and H.T.W. Hardinge. Kent finished twelfth in the County Championship with 8 wins, 16 defeats and 4 draws. Les Ames hit a record 201 not out versus Worcestershire at Gillingham.

Born in Chartham in 1915, Arthur Fagg created a unique world record while playing against Essex at Castle Park, Colchester, in 1938 when he recorded two double centuries in the same match – 244 and 202 not out. He represented Kent between 1932 and 1957 in 414 matches, scoring 26,072 runs (av. 36.06) with a top score of 269 not out versus Nottinghamshire at Trent Bridge in 1953. Arthur scored 55 centuries for the county, held 411 catches and managed 7 stumpings. He died at Tunbridge Wells in 1977.

Kent CCC, 1938. From left to right, back row: N.W. Harding, L.E.G. Ames, P.R. Sunnunks, A.E. Watt, A.E. Fagg, T.W. Spencer, D.V.P. Wright, L.J. Todd. Front row: W.H.V. Levett, B.H. Valentine, F.G.H. Chalk (captain), F.E. Woolley, J.D.W. Davies. Kent finished ninth in the County Championship with 8 wins, 14 defeats and 6 draws and the season saw a number of records established. Kent scored 377 against the touring Australians at Canterbury their highest innings total against the baggy green caps. Arthur Fagg hit his two double centuries against Essex and Kent recorded their highest innings total against Worcestershire with a score of 602 for 7 declared at Dudley.

The carpet bedding display at The Leas during the 1938 Folkestone Cricket Festival. It depicts the England versus Australia Test series played during that summer in England.

Kent CCC, 1946. The team included: R.R. Dovey, T.W. Spencer, C.C. Lewis, W.H.V. Levett, J.D.W. Davies, B.H. Valentine (captain), L.E.G. Ames and L.J. Todd. Kent finished in equal sixth position in the County Championship with 11 wins, 8 defeats and 7 draws.

Kent CCC, 1947. From left to right, back row: F. Ridgway, B.R. Edrich, J.W. Martin, R.R. Dovey, C. Lewis. Front row: D.V.P. Wright, E. Crush, L.E.G. Ames, B.H. Valentine (captain), L.J. Todd, A.E. Fagg, T.G. Evans. Kent finished fourth in the County Championship with 12 wins, 8 defeats and 6 draws.

Douglas Wright played 397 matches for Kent, having made his county debut in 1932. He took 1,709 wickets (av. 22.68) with a best performance of 9 for 47 versus Gloucestershire at Bristol in 1939 and he scored 5,074 runs (av. 12.46) with a top score of 84 not out versus Hampshire at Southampton, also in 1939. He held a total of 152 catches. A right-arm leg-spin bowler he bowled with a bounding run which was often compared with a kangaroo's hopping. In 1937 he took 111 wickets (av. 27.19) and went on to make his Test debut versus Australia at Trent Bridge in 1938. He took a world record 7 hat-tricks during his career and he toured South Africa and Australia twice. He played 34 Tests, taking 108 wickets (av. 39.11) with a best performance of 7 for 105 versus Australia at Sydney in 1946/47 when not one of the Aussie batsman could master his bowling action. In 1947 he took 142 wickets (av. 19.01), including 15 for 173 versus Sussex at Hastings. In 1954 Wright became the first professional captain of Kent and led the county until 1956. After retiring he became the cricket professional at Charterhouse School, Surrey. He died in Canterbury in 1998.

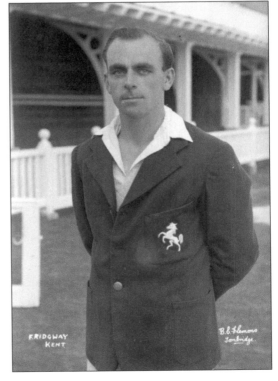

Born in Stockport in 1923, Fred Ridgway played 298 matches for the county between 1946 and 1961. He scored 3,812 runs (av. 11.14) with a top score of 94 and he took 955 wickets (av. 23.81) with a best bowling performance of 8 for 39 against Nottinghamshire at Dover in 1950 and Lancashire at Dartford in 1960.

TUNBRIDGE WELLS CRICKET WEEK - 1947

KENT v. SUSSEX, Nevill Ground, Tunbridge Wells, Saturday, Monday & Tuesday, 28th, 30th June & 1st July, 1947.

	KENT. 1st INNINGS	2ND INNINGS		SUSSEX 1ST INNINGS	2ND INNINGS
1	Todd L J b. Carey 9		1 †S C Griffith Dovey 36	
2	Fagg A lbw. Oakes (C)		2 Oakes J c. Harding 3	
3	Hearn P c. Griffiths b. Oakes (C) 15		3 Parks H W c b. Dovey 7	
4	G F Anson c. Oakes (C) b. Carey 11		4 Cox G c. Anson b. Dovey 0	
5	*B H Valentine b. Cornford 13		5 Oakes C	
6	†Evans T G b. Parks b. Cox 14		6 *H T Bartlett c. Wright 7	
7	Edrich B not out 16		7 Langridge John b. Wright 33	
8	Dovey R R b. Oakes (C)		8 A P Doggart	
9	Wright D V P b. Carey		9 Smith D	
10	Harding N W b. Carey 0		10 Carey P	
11	J W Martin b. Cornford 0		11 Cornford J	
	Byes , l-byes I , no-balls , wides 8	Byes , l-b , n-b , w		Byes , l-byes , no-balls , wides	Byes , l-b , n-b , w
	Total 149	Total		Total	Total

1st Inns.—1 for 12, 2-54, 3-84, 4-107, 5-106, 6-127, 7-136, 8-148, 9-148
2nd Inns.—1 for ..., 2-..., 3-..., 4-..., 5-..., 6-..., 7-..., 8-..., 9-...

1st Inns.—1 for 50, 2-60, 3-..., 4-..., 5-..., 6-..., 7-..., 8-..., 9-...
2nd Inns.—1 for ..., 2-..., 3-..., 4-..., 5-..., 6-..., 7-..., 8-..., 9-...

Umpires—E Cooke & G M Lee   *Denotes Captain.   †Denotes Wkt.-kpr.   Scorers—W Locke & E Hosking   Kent won the toss.

Bowler	Overs	Mds.	Rns.	Wkt.	W.	N.B.	Bowler	Overs Mds. Rns.Wkt. W. N.B.	Bowler	Overs	Mds.	Rns.	Wkt.	W.	N.B.	Bowler	Overs Mds. Rns.Wkt. W. N.B.
Carey									Martin								
Cornford		36		2					Harding								
Cox		2A	1						Wright								
Oakes (C)		8		3					Dovey								
Smith																	
Oakes (J)		3	0														

Hours of Play—1st Day 11.30 ; Lunch 1.30 ; Draw 6 30   2nd Day 11 30 ; Lunch 1.30 ; Draw 6 30 ;   3rd Day 11.30 ; Lunch 1.30 ; Draw 6 0 or 6.30

Membership

The Kent County Cricket Club welcomes new Members. Subscriptions: £1 11s. 6d., £2 2s. 0d. and £3 3s. 0d.; Juveniles (up to the age of 18) £1. For full particulars apply to the Secretary, St. Lawrence Ground, Canterbury, or to any K.C.C.C. official on the Ground. There are no formalities about joining the Club.

The Centenary of the Canterbury Week will be held in 1948.
L. J. Todd's Benefit, Aug. 2, 4, 5, Kent v. Hants., at Canterbury.
To avoid frequent stoppages of play, Car Owners are asked kindly to cover their windscreens when the sun gets into a position likely to cause dazzle.
The K.C.C.C. Year Book can be purchased on the ground, price 2s. 6d.

Next Matches in Kent

At Tunbridge Wells :—
Kent v. Yorkshire, July 2nd, 3rd and 4th.
At Blackheath :—
Kent v. Surrey, July 19th, 21st and 22nd.
At Maidstone :—
Kent v. Somersetshire, July 23rd, 24th and 25th.
Kent v. Essex, July 26th, 28th and 29th.

Programme - 3d.   Printed on the ground by Messrs. Clements & Son (Tun. Wells) Ltd., Grove Hill Road, Tun. Wells, from whom complete cards may be obtained after each day's play.

A partly completed scorecard for the Kent versus Sussex County Championship match staged at the Nevill Cricket Ground between 28 June and 1 July as part of the Tunbridge Wells Cricket Week of 1947. The match scores were Kent 149 and 256, Sussex 126 and 283 for 5, with John Langridge guiding Sussex home by 6 wickets despite Doug Wright taking match figures of 8 for 155.

Making his Kent debut against Derbyshire at the Bat and Ball Ground, Gravesend, in 1939, Godfrey Evans had boxed three fights at welterweight before deciding on a career in cricket. Representing Kent until 1967 he was an exceptional 'Cockney' wicketkeeper with fine agility, balance and anticipation. A right-handed batsman who played 258 matches for Kent, he scored 9,325 runs (av. 21.38) with 4 hundreds and a top score of 144 versus Somerset at Taunton in 1952. He held 451 catches and took 103 stumpings. He represented the Army during wartime matches at Lord's and was capped in 1946; he made his England debut versus India at Kennington Oval and played the last of his 91 Tests at Lord's in 1959. He toured abroad 8 times and made 2 Test centuries (both of 104) versus the West Indies at Old Trafford in 1950 and India at Lord's in 1952. He collected 173 catches and 46 stumpings and his best series was in 1956/57 versus South Africa, when he collected 20 dismissals. He scored 2,439 Test runs (av. 20.49) and was the first wicketkeeper to achieve 2,000 runs and 200 dismissals. He died in 1999.

Les Ames in close up, as featured in Len Hutton's benefit souvenir booklet of 1949.

Kent CCC, 1949. From left to right, back row: P. Hearn, T.G. Evans, B.R. Edrich, E. Crush, R.R. Dovey, A.H. Phebey, F. Ridgway. Front row: A.E. Fagg, L.E.G. Ames, D.G. Clark (captain), L.J. Todd, D.V.P. Wright. Kent finished in equal thirteenth place in the County Championship with 7 wins, 15 defeats and 4 draws. They recorded their lowest innings total against Glamorgan, with 49 at the St Helen's Ground in Swansea.

Born in 1911, Jack Davies studied at Tonbridge where he represented the school's cricket team between 1927 and 1930. He was captain of the school during his last year before he went up to Cambridge. He represented the university between 1933 and 1934 and made his Kent debut in 1934. A right-handed batsman, he played 99 matches for the county, scoring 4,059 runs (av. 25.36) with a top score of 168 versus Worcestershire at Worcester in 1946. He took 197 wickets (av. 29.81) with a best haul of 7 for 20 with his slow off-break bowling and he held 55 catches – usually at cover point. He later went on to act as secretary of Cambridge University Cricket Club at Fenner's and was often seen at the ground. He also played rugby for Blackheath and Kent. Davies later acted as MCC president and died at Cambridge in 1996.

H.A PAWSON
KENT

Tony Pawson was the son of A.G. (Worcestershire) and nephew of A.C. (Oxford University). Born in Chertsey in 1921, he was a stylish right-handed batsman, useful off-break bowler and good fieldsman, playing 43 matches for the county between 1946 and 1953. He attained Blues at Oxford in 1947 and 1948, captaining the Dark Blues in his second season. He scored 2,100 runs (av. 33.33) with a top score of 137 for the county versus Essex at Maidstone in 1950, took 4 wickets (av. 32.75) and held 16 catches. He was a keen footballer and, like a few other Kent cricketers, played for Charlton Athletic. A highly respected cricket writer, he was awarded an OBE for services to fishing, his second sporting love.

Playing his early cricket at Mill Hill and Oxford University between 1936 and 1938, William Murray-Wood captained the county in 1952 and 1953. He was a hard-hitting, middle-order, right-handed batsman and useful leg-break bowler who represented Kent in 77 matches from 1936 to 1953. On his first-class debut while at Oxford he scored 106 not out against Gloucestershire at the University Parks in 1936. He scored 1,658 runs (av. 13.59) with a top score of 107 versus Sussex at Tunbridge Wells in 1952, took 47 wickets (av. 40.70) and he held 29 catches. He toured abroad twice with a Combined Universities side to Jamaica in 1938/39 and with Stuart Surridge to Bermuda in 1961. He died in Southwark in 1968.

Alan Dixon was born in Dartford in 1933. He played 378 matches for Kent between 1950 and 1970 as a right-arm opening bowler and middle-order, right-handed batsman. He bagged 929 wickets (av. 25.69) with a best performance of 8 for 61 versus Northamptonshire at Dover in 1964 and scored 9,561 runs (av. 18.93) with a highest innings of 125 not out. During a Gillette Cup match with Surrey at The Oval he took 7 for 15 in 1967, en route to Kent winning the trophy for the first time. He took 100 wickets in a season on three occasions with a best seasonal return of 122 wickets (av. 23.89) in 1964.

Four
Cowdrey, Denness and the Gillette Cup Kings

Kent CCC, 1950. From left to right, back row: F. Ridgway, P. Hearn, A.H. Phebey, E. Crush, R.R. Dovey, B.R. Edrich, T.G. Evans. Front row: D.V.P. Wright, L.E.G. Ames, D.G. Clark (captain), L.J. Todd, A.E. Fagg. Kent finished ninth in the County Championship with 6 wins, 12 defeats, 9 draws and a tied match.

Kent CCC, 1951, The side included: B.R. Edrich, P. Hearn, M.C. Cowdrey, R.R. Dovey, F. Ridgway, D.V.P. Wright, L.E.G. Ames, D.G. Clark (captain), A.E. Fagg, T.G. Evans. Kent finished in sixteenth place in the County Championship with 4 wins, 15 defeats and 9 draws. During the match with Derbyshire at Folkestone, Fred Ridgway took 4 wickets with 4 balls.

Kent CCC, 1952. The team included: B.R. Edrich, A.H. Phebey, R.R. Dovey, F. Ridgway, T.G. Evans, A.E. Fagg, W. Murray-Wood (captain), D.V.P. Wright and W.H.V. Levett. Kent finished fifteenth in the County Championship with 5 wins, 15 defeats and 8 draws.

Kent CCC, 1955. From left to right, back row: A.L. Dixon, R.C. Wilson, J.C.T. Page, P. Hearn, J.S. Pettiford, A.H. Phebey, A.F. Brazier. Front row: A.C. Shirreff, A.E. Fagg, D.V.P. Wright (captain), T.G. Evans, F. Ridgway. Kent finished thirteenth in the County Championship with 9 wins, 12 defeats and 7 draws.

Kent CCC, 1957. From left to right, back row: R.C. Wilson, D.J. Halfyard, C.C. Page, J. Pettiford, S.E. Leary, B.E. Disbury, J.F. Pretlove. Front row: A.H. Phebey, D.V.P. Wright, M.C. Cowdrey (captain), T.G. Evans, F. Ridgway. Kent finished fourteenth in the County Championship with 6 wins, 13 defeats and 9 draws.

Given the initials 'MCC' by his father, who represented the Europeans versus India in 1926/27, Colin Cowdrey was coached by Ewart Astill at Tonbridge School and was the youngest player (at thirteen years old) to play at Lord's. At nineteen he became the youngest player to collect a Kent cap. He represented Kent for twenty-six years and was a prolific right-handed middle-order batsman of the highest quality, playing 402 matches and scoring 23,779 runs (av. 42.01) with 58 centuries and a top score of 250 versus Essex at Blackheath in 1959. He was Kent's captain between 1957 and 1971. Cowdrey held 406 catches and took 27 wickets (av. 47.59) with a best performance of 4 for 22. He made his Test debut in 1954/55 versus Australia at Brisbane and went on to play in a total of 114 Tests, scoring 7,624 runs (av. 44.06) with 22 centuries. He made 16 tours abroad and his highest score was 182 versus Pakistan at Kennington Oval in 1962. He captained England in 27 Tests with 8 victories. After a career total of 42,719 runs with 107 centuries, Colin Cowdrey was knighted for his services to cricket in 1992 and named a lord in 1996. He was president of MCC in 1987/88 and the ICC between 1993 and 1995.

Born locally at Bapchild near Faversham in 1928, Robert 'Bob' Wilson was an attractive left-handed top-order batsman and an excellent outfielder. He represented the county between 1952 and 1967 in 365 matches, scoring 19,458 runs (av. 32.10) with a highest innings of 159 not out versus Northamptonshire at Kettering in 1963, when he added a record 283 for the third wicket with Stuart Leary (who was also making his career best score for the county at the time).

David Halfyard was born in Winchmore Hill in 1931 and represented the county in 185 matches between 1956 and 1964. He scored 2,538 runs (av. 10.44) with a top score of 79 and he bagged 769 wickets (av. 24.47) with a best haul of 9 for 39 versus Glamorgan at Neath in 1957. He later joined Nottinghamshire, for whom he played 77 matches between 1968 and 1970, and was appointed a first-class umpire in 1967.

A stylish opening batsman and excellent fieldsman, Arthur Phebey was born in Catford in 1924. He played 320 matches for the county between 1946 and 1961, during which time he scored 14,299 runs (av. 25.90) with 12 centuries and a top score of 157 versus Gloucestershire at Bristol in 1958. A useful footballer, he played inside right for both Dulwich Hamlet and Hendon.

KENT TEAM 1959

C. PAGE.   J. PRODGER.   A. BROWN.   D. HALFYARD.   P. JONES.   A. DIXON.   R. WILSON.

F. RIDGWAY.   G. EVANS.   C. COWDREY (CAPT.)   A. PHEBEY.   J. PETTIFORD.   J. PRETLOVE.

Kent CCC, 1959. From left to right, back row: C.C. Page, J.M. Prodger, A. Brown, D.J. Halfyard, P.H. Jones, A. L. Dixon, R.C. Wilson. Front row: F. Ridgway, T.G. Evans, M.C. Cowdrey (captain), A.H. Phebey, J. Pettiford, J.F. Pretlove. Kent finished thirteenth in the County Championship with 8 wins, 12 defeats and 8 draws.

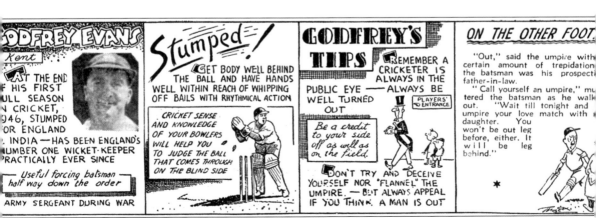

Godfrey Evans in close-up, as featured in Jack Parker's benefit souvenir booklet of 1950.

John Prodger was born at Forest Hill in 1935 and was a solid right-handed batsman who made his debut for the county against Lancashire at Old Trafford in 1956. He played 151 matches for Kent between 1956 and 1967, scoring 4,831 runs (av. 20.38) with a top score of 170 not out versus Essex at Maidstone in 1961. He held 170 catches, mostly at slip where he was a more than useful fieldsman.

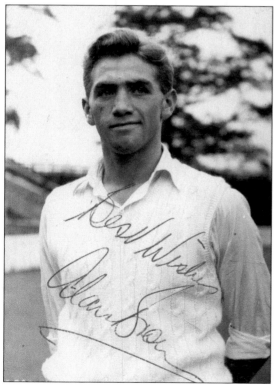

Born in Nottinghamshire in 1935, right-arm quickie Alan Brown represented the county from 1957 until 1970, playing a total of 237 matches for the club. He took 707 wickets (av. 24.80) with a best performance of 8 for 47 versus Warwickshire at the Griff & Coton Ground, Nuneaton, in 1969. He scored 2,120 runs (av. 9.63) with a highest innings of 81 against Glamorgan at Folkestone in 1968.

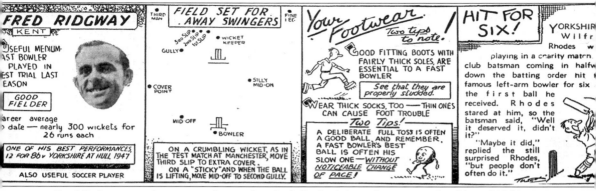

Fred Ridgway in close-up, as featured in Jack Parker's benefit souvenir booklet of 1950.

Kent CCC, 1963. From left to right, back row: C. Lewis (scorer), A.W. Catt, B.W. Luckhurst, D.W. Baker, M.H. Denness, D.L. Underwood, L.E.G. Ames (manager). Front row: A. Brown, P.H. Jones, R.C. Wilson, M.C. Cowdrey (captain), P.E. Richardson, S.E. Leary, A.L. Dixon. Kent finished thirteenth in the County Championship with 4 wins, 6 defeats and 18 draws.

Kent CCC, 1960. From left to right, back row: P.E. Richardson, R.W. Wilkinson, P.H. Jones, C.C. Page, D.J. Halfyard, A. L. Dixon, A.W. Catt, C.C. Lewis (coach). Front row: S.E. Leary, F. Ridgway, M.C. Cowdrey (captain), L.E.G. Ames (manager), A.H. Phebey, R.C. Wilson. Kent finished tenth in the County Championship with 7 wins, 7 defeats and 14 draws. At the Nevill Ground in Tunbridge Wells, Kent's home match with Worcestershire was completed on the first day when Kent (187) beat Worcestershire (25 and 61) by an innings and 101 runs.

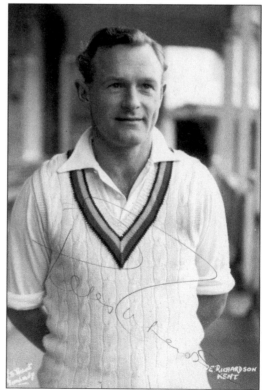

Born in Hereford in 1931, Peter Richardson – brother of D.W. (Worcestershire) and B.A. (Warwickshire) – represented Kent in 162 matches between 1959 and 1965. An excellent left-handed opening batsman and a splendid fieldsman, he represented Worcestershire 161 times between 1949 and 1958 prior to his arrival in the Garden of England. He scored 9,975 runs (av. 35.88) for Kent with 18 centuries, of which his best was 172 versus Yorkshire at Middlesborough in 1962. Richardson took 4 wickets (av. 41.00) with a best of 2 for 32 and held 96 catches, usually at cover point. He played 34 Tests for England and toured abroad between 1955/56 and 1964/65 with various sides, during which time he scored 2,061 runs (av. 37.47) with a top score of 126.

A masterful all-rounder, Stuart Leary was born in Cape Town in 1933. He was an effective right-handed middle-order batsman, good leg-break bowler and excellent close fieldsman. He made his county debut against Essex at Ilford's Valentine's Park in 1951 and went on to play 381 matches until his retirement from the game in 1971. He scored 16,169 runs (av. 30.79) with a top score of 158 versus Northamptonshire at Kettering in 1963. He took 160 wickets (av. 33.67), with a best performance of 5 for 22 versus Glamorgan at Swansea in 1961, and held 362 catches. He played League football, as a centre forward, for Charlton Athletic and Queen's Park Rangers. Tragically, in 1988 this gifted sportsman took his own life on Table Mountain, South Africa.

Kent CCC, 1961. From left to right, back row: P.H. Jones, A.L. Dixon, D.J. Halfyard, D.M. Sayer, A. Brown, J.M. Prodger, A.W. Catt, C. Lewis (coach). Front row: P.E. Richardson, S.E. Leary, R.C. Wilson, M.C. Cowdrey (captain), A.H. Phebey, D.G. Ufton, F. Ridgway. Kent finished eleventh in the County Championship with 7 wins, 9 defeats and 12 draws. During the fixture with Gloucestershire at Cheltenham, John Prodger took a record 8 catches in a match.

A left-handed lower-order batsman and wicketkeeper, Derek Ufton represented the county between 1949 and 1962. He played 148 matches, scoring 3,915 runs (av. 20.18) with a top score of 119 not out versus Sussex at Hastings in 1964. He also held 269 catches and took 44 stumpings. A notable soccer player, he represented Charlton Athletic and England at centre-half.

Kent CCC, 1967. From left to right, standing: A.P.E. Knott, M.H. Denness, J.N. Shepherd, D.L. Underwood, D. Sayer, J.N. Graham, M.C. Cowdrey (captain), S.E. Leary, A.G.E. Ealham, A.L. Dixon, A. Brown. Kent finished as runners-up in the County Championship with 11 wins, 3 defeats and 13 draws. In the course of this successful season, Kent dismissed Hampshire for a meagre 31 at The Mote in Maidstone. During the tour match with the Pakistanis at the St Lawrence Ground, Derek Underwood took 7 for 78 in an innings (match analysis of 10 for 152). Kent won the Gillette Cup for the first time when Somerset were defeated at Lord's.

Derek 'Deadly' Underwood, a slow-medium left-arm spinner, took 101 wickets (av. 21.12) in 1963 – his first county season – thus becoming the youngest player ever to take 100 wickets in his debut season. This included 4 for 40 in his first match for Kent, against Yorkshire, at The Circle in Hull. Playing 519 matches for the county, he took 1,952 wickets (av. 19.25), with a best performance of 9 for 28 versus Sussex at Hastings in 1964, and scored 3,793 runs (av. 9.87) with a top score of 111 versus Sussex at Hastings in 1984. In 1966 he took 157 wickets and made the first of his 86 Test appearances versus West Indies at Trent Bridge. He toured abroad 11 times and took 297 wickets (av. 25.83) with a best performance of 8 for 51 versus Pakistan at Lord's in 1974. Batting at no. 11, he scored 937 runs (av. 11.56) for England, with a highest score of 45 not out versus Australia at Headingley in 1968. He joined World Series Cricket in 1977 and later toured South Africa with the rebel England XI in 1981/82. In all first-class matches he took 2,465 wickets – the fourteenth highest total of all time. He was awarded the MBE for services to cricket and since retiring he has been active with the Primary Club and the Royal Brussels CC in Belgium.

Mike Denness was born at Bellshill near Glasgow. A right-handed opening batsman and fine fielder, he was coached by Charlie Oakes at Ayr CC and in 1959 he became the first schoolboy to be capped by Scotland when he made his first-class debut against Ireland. Recommended by Jim Allan for a trial with Kent, he made his county debut in 1962 versus Essex. In 1967 he won the Gillette Cup final Man of the Match award after the game with Somerset at Lord's and was half of the best opening partnership on the county circuit – Denness and Brian Luckhurst scoring 3,000 runs between them. A determined leader, he became only the second Scotsman (after Ian Peebles of Middlesex) to captain a county, leading Kent from 1972 to 1976. He made his Test debut against New Zealand at The Oval in 1969 and he captained England in 19 of his 28 Tests. He scored 1,667 runs (av. 39.69) with a top score of 188 versus Australia at Melbourne in 1974/75. He represented Kent in 333 matches, scoring 17,047 runs (av. 32.90) with 21 hundreds and holding 308 catches. Denness led Kent to six one-day trophies before departing for Essex in 1977.

Born in Sittingbourne, Brian Luckhurst was a right-handed top-order batsman and excellent backward square-leg fielder, who represented the Army and Combined Services before making his Kent debut versus Worcestershire in 1958. However, he did not become a regular First XI player until 1962. In 1965 he began a long-standing opening partnership with Mike Denness, of which his most productive season was 1969 when he scored 1,914 runs (av. 47.85). He represented England in 21 Tests, scoring 1,298 runs (av. 36.05) with a top score of 131 versus Australia at Perth in 1970/71 and he toured abroad twice to Australia in 1970/71 and 1974/75. He played a total of 335 matches for Kent, scoring 19,096 runs (av. 38.00), exceeding 1,000 runs in a season 14 times and hitting 39 centuries. His highest score was 215 versus Derbyshire at Derby in 1973. As a slow left-arm orthodox spinner he took 61 wickets (av. 42.90) with a best performance of 4 for 32 versus Somerset at Gravesend in 1962. Brian later acted as cricket administrator of the county club and since retiring continues to serve the club by running the bar and sports complex in the Ames Levett Indoor Cricket School on the St Lawrence Ground.

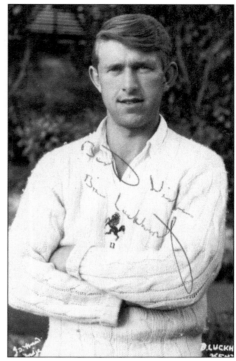

Kent CCC, 1969. From left to right, back row: C. Lewis (scorer), A.P.E. Knott, R.A. Woolmer, J.C.J. Dye, J.N. Graham, D.L. Underwood, J.N. Shepherd, Asif Iqbal, A.G.E. Ealham. Front row: A. Brown, M.H. Denness, A.L. Dixon, M.C. Cowdrey (captain), L.E.G. Ames (manager), S.E. Leary, B.W. Luckhurst. Kent finished tenth in the County Championship with 4 wins, 6 defeats and 14 draws.

Having been persuaded by his father, a wicketkeeper with Belvedere CC, to play cricket rather than stay at school it is hardly surprising that Alan Knott chose cricket and made his debut for Kent against Cambridge University at Folkestone in 1964. Capped in his second season, he went on to represent the county in 349 matches, scoring 11,339 runs (av. 27.58) with 9 centuries and a top score of 144 versus Sussex at Canterbury in 1976. He took a total of 828 catches and 87 stumpings for the county. Making his Test debut in 1967 versus Pakistan at Trent Bridge, he went on to appear 95 times for England. Knott was renowned for his superb acrobatic catching ability as well as his deadly alliance with Kent colleague Derek Underwood, which yielded 269 victims. He scored 4,389 runs (av. 32.75) with 5 centuries – which frequently came when England were in trouble. Underwood was the first wicketkeeper after Les Ames to score a century in a Test match versus Australia when he notched up 135 at Trent Bridge in 1977. He later joined World Series cricket. Since retiring he has acted as an observer for the TCCB and wicketkeeping coach for England.

Born in Barbados in 1943, John Shepherd joined
Kent in 1965 and, after qualifying by representing
the St Lawrence club, made his Kent debut in
1966. A hard-hitting right-hand middle-order
batsman and right-arm fast-medium bowler, he
scored 13,334 runs (av. 26.44) with 10 centuries
and a highest score of 170 versus Northamptonshire
at Folkestone in 1968. He took 1,155 wickets (av.
27.64) with a best innings performance of 8 for 40
for the West Indians versus Gloucestershire at
Bristol in 1969 and best match figures of 15 for
147 versus Sussex at Hove in 1975. He
represented his native West Indies in 7 Tests,
scoring 77 runs (av. 9.62), with a highest score of
32 versus England at Lord's in 1969, and he took
19 wickets (av. 25.21) with best figures of 5 for
104 versus England at Old Trafford in 1969. His
best season was 1968, when he accumulated 1,157
runs (av. 29.66) and took 96 wickets (av. 18.72).
He played for Rhodesia and became the first black
cricketer to play in the Currie Cup in South
Africa in 1975/76. After leaving Kent he played
for Gloucestershire from 1982 to 1987. Since
retiring he has concentrated on coaching and he
is now the master in charge of cricket at
Eastbourne College.

Born in Northumberland in 1943, John
Graham represented the county between
1967 and 1977 in 186 matches. A right-arm
medium-pace bowler, he bagged 600
wickets (av. 22.43) with a best performance
of 8 for 20 versus Essex at Brentwood in
1969. As a right-handed tail-end batsman
he scored 404 runs (av. 3.88) with a top
score of 23.

CANTERBURY — August 26th, 27th and 28th 1964
KENT v AUSTRALIANS
Hours of Play: 1st day 11.30-6.30 2nd day 11.30-7 3rd day 11.00-4.30
Kent won the toss and elected to bat

KENT	1st innings	2nd innings
1 P E Richardson lbw b Hawke	111	
2 E W J Fillary c Burge b Corling	46	c and b O'Neill ... 25
3 R C Wilson c Redpath b Hawke	45	
†4 M C Cowdrey c Grout b Redpath	90	
5 J M Prodger b Hawke	13	
6 B W Luckhurst not out	2	
7 A L Dixon not out	13	
‡8 A Knott c Grout b Redpath	4	
9 D Underwood		
10 D M Sayer		
11 J C Dye		
	b 10 lb 6 nb 7 23	Total
	Total (for 6 wkts dec) 346	

Runs at fall of wicket:—
1st Innings   1-154 2-167 3-267 4-305 5-322 6-338 7-   8-   9-   10-
2nd Innings   1-01 2-   3-   4-   5-   6-   7-   8-   9-   10-

Bowling Analysis	O	M	R	W	Wd	Nb	O	M	R	W	Wd	Nb
Hawke	28	6	75	3								
Corling	13	4	40	1	7							
Veivers	19	2	52	0								
Martin	21	4	83	0								
O'Neill	5	0	18	0								
Booth	1	0	5	0								
Potter	2	0	9	0								
Redpath	6	0	33	2								

AUSTRALIANS	1st Innings	2nd Innings
1 W M Lawry c Luckhurst b Dye	55	
2 I R Redpath b Sayer	13	
3 J Potter c Sayer b Underwood	75	
4 N C O'Neill c Knott b Dixon	37	
5 P J Burge c Knott b Underwood	27	
†6 B C Booth c and b Underwood	27	
7 T R Veivers c Knott b Underwood	79	
8 J W Martin not out	11	
‡9 A T W Grout c Dye b Underwood	8	
10 N J N Hawke not out	13	
11 G E Corling		
	lb 1 Nb 1 2	Total
	Total (for 8 wkts dec) 354	

Runs at fall of wicket:—
1st Innings   1-21 2-102 3-176 4-193 5-215 6-269 7-281 8-338 9-   10-
2nd Innings   1-   2-   3-   4-   5-   6-   7-   8-   9-   10-

Bowling Analysis	O	M	R	W	Wd	Nb	O	M	R	W	Wd	Nb
Dye	11	4	24	1								
Sayer	13	1	53	1								
Underwood	26	11	100	5								
Fillary	20	2	87	0	1							
Dixon	23	3	78	1								
Luckhurst	2	0	19	0								

Intervals
Lunch 1.30-2.10
Tea usually 4.30

Umpires:
P. A. Gibb
J. H. Parks

Scorers:
C. Lewis
D. Sherwood

The teams are being entertained to lunch and tea today by Bagnall Harvey, Esq.

Appendix 'H'
HISTORY OF KENT CRICKET
Now on Sale 5/-

†Captain
‡Wicketkeeper

New ball due after 85 overs.

MEMBERSHIP
Join the K.C.C.C., details can be obtained from the office on the ground.

PORTABLE RADIOS
The Committee does not wish to prohibit the use of portable radio sets on Kent Grounds, but requests that they be not used during the hours of play.

The Kent County Cricket Annual is available on the ground price 2/6.

Completed Cards at end of each day's play.

Printed on the Ground by J. A. Jennings, Ltd., Canterbury.

A partly printed up scorecard of the Kent versus Australians tour match at the St Lawrence ground between 26 and 28 August 1964. The match scores were Kent 346 for 6 declared (P.E. Richardson 111, M.C. Cowdrey 90, N.J.N. Hawke 3 for 75) and 258 for 3 (P.E. Richardson 115, M.C. Cowdrey 50 not out, J.W. Martin 2 for 67), the Australians 354 for 8 declared (T.R. Veivers 79, J. Potter 75, W.M. Lawry 55, D.L. Underwood 5 for 100) and 252 for 2 (N.C. O'Neill 110, W.M. Lawry 101 not out, J.C.J. Dye 1 for 22). The touring Australians won by 8 wickets.

Born in Norfolk in 1943, David Nicholls was a reliable left-handed middle-order batsman, occasional seam bowler and often wicketkeeper. He made his debut for the county in 1960, aged 16 years and 183 days, and was the second youngest to play for the county club after H.T.W. Hardinge. Nicholls went on to play 201 matches for the county, scoring 7,026 runs (av. 22.23). His highest score for Kent was 211 versus Derbyshire at Folkestone in 1963. He took 339 dismissals (326 catches and 13 stumpings) during his Kent career, which lasted from 1960 to 1977.

THE GILLETTE CRICKET CUP FINAL
KENT v SOMERSET
AT LORD'S

OFFICIAL SOUVENIR PROGRAMME

2/6

SATURDAY 2nd. SEPTEMBER 1967

This official souvenir programme was issued on Saturday 2 September 1967 for the Gillette Cup final match between Kent and Somerset at Lord's. Kent became Gillette Cup winners for the first time thanks to a 32-run victory. Kent scored 193 all out in 59.4 overs with batsman Brian Luckhurst (54 runs), Mike Denness (50) and John Shepherd (30) the main run scorers. Bill Alley and Roy Palmer were the leading wicket takers for Somerset with 3 for 22 and 3 for 53 respectively. In reply, Somerset made 161 all out in 54.5 overs with Peter Robinson (48) and Graham Burgess (27) the highest scoring batsman. Spinner Derek Underwood was the best Kent bowler with 3 for 41.

Graham Johnson was born in Beckenham in 1946 and he represented Kent in 376 matches between 1965 and 1985. As a right-handed middle-order batsman he scored 12,509 runs (av. 24.77) with a top score of 168 against Surrey at The Oval in 1976. A useful off-break bowler, he bagged 560 wickets (av. 30.93) with a best haul of 7 for 76 and was also a good fieldsman, picking up 302 catches, usually at slip.

Born in Kanpur, India, Bob Woolmer was the son of a British businessman who had captained Uttar Pradesh. Educated at Skinners School in Tonbridge, his club was Tunbridge Wells CC before he joined the Kent staff thanks to Colin Page. He scored an unbeaten 50 on his county debut versus Essex at Maidstone in 1968 and was awarded his county cap in 1970. He made his Test debut versus Australia at Lord's in 1975 and at The Oval in the sixth Test of the series scored 149 in 6 hours 34 minutes (which was the slowest century by an Englishman in an Ashes series). A graceful right-handed batsman and useful right-arm medium-pace bowler, he played 279 matches for Kent, scoring 12,634 runs (av. 35.09) with 28 centuries and a top score of 203 versus Sussex at Tunbridge Wells in 1982. He took 334 wickets (av. 23.38), with a best performance of 7 for 47 versus Sussex at Canterbury in 1969, and held 195 catches. Like Derek Underwood and Alan Knott, he joined Kerry Packer's World Series cricket circus in 1977, but not before he had played in 19 Tests, scoring 1,059 runs (av. 33.09). Since retiring he has acted as cricket manager for Warwickshire CCC and the South Africa national side.

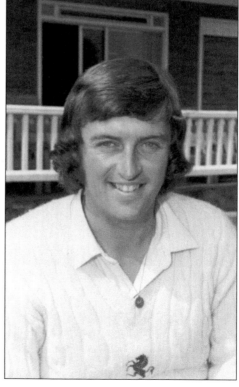

Five

The Glory Years

Pilgrim Philatelics of Canterbury produced a first day cover, which was posted at the St Lawrence Cricket Ground on 30 May 1970 to celebrate the centenary of the Kent County Cricket Club.

Kent CCC, 1970. Kent finished first in the County Championship, winning it for the fifth time in the county's history. They won 9, lost 5 and drew 10 of their games. From left to right, back row: L. Kilby (physiotherapist), R.A. Woolmer, J.N. Shepherd, A. Brown, J.N. Graham, J.C.J. Dye, G.W. Johnson, Asif Iqbal, J.C.T. Page, C. Lewis (scorer). Front row: D. Nicholls, A.P.E. Knott, D.L. Underwood, M.H. Denness, M.C. Cowdrey (captain), L.E.G. Ames (manager), S.E. Leary, B.W. Luckhurst, A.G.E. Ealham.

A first day cover produced by Stamp Publicity of Worthing and posted at Lord's on 4 September 1971 to celebrate the 1971 Gillette Cup final, in which Lancashire beat Kent by 3 wickets. The match scores were Lancashire 224 for 7 in 60 overs (Clive Lloyd 66, David Lloyd 38, John Dye 2 for 51) and Kent 200 all out in 56.2 overs (Asif Iqbal 89, Mike Denness 29, Peter Lever 3 for 24). Asif Iqbal won the Man of the Match award despite Lancashire winning by 24 runs.

The programme for the Gillette Cup final between Kent and Lancashire at Lord's, Saturday 4 September 1971.

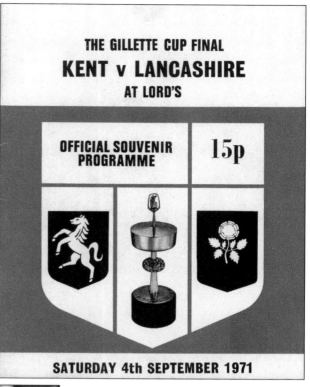

THE GILLETTE CUP FINAL
KENT v LANCASHIRE
AT LORD'S

OFFICIAL SOUVENIR PROGRAMME

15p

SATURDAY 4th SEPTEMBER 1971

West Indian Test all-rounder Bernard Julien joined the county in 1970 and played for the club until 1977, during which time he played 80 matches. He scored 2,057 runs (av. 21.88) with a top score of 98 and took 198 wickets (av. 26.54) with a best haul of 7 for 66.

Kent CCC, 1972. From left to right, back row: D. Nicholls, B.D. Julien, R.A. Woolmer, G.W. Johnson, J.N. Graham, R.B. Elms, D.Laycock, A.G.E. Ealham. Front row: Asif Iqbal, J.C.T. Page, D.L. Underwood, M.C. Cowdrey, M.H. Denness (captain), L.E.G. Ames (manager), B.W. Luckhurst, A.P.E. Knott, J.N. Shepherd. Kent finished as runners-up in the County Championship with 7 wins, 4 defeats and 9 draws. Kent won the John Player Sunday League for the first time.

A first day cover produced by Stamp Publicity of Worthing and posted at Lord's on 21 July 1973 to celebrate the 1973 Benson & Hedges Cup final, in which Kent beat Worcestershire by 39 runs. Asif Iqbal won the Man of the Match award for his 59 runs and 4 wickets for 43 runs.

Kent CCC, 1973. From left to right: D. Nicholls, D.L. Underwood, J.N. Shepherd, Asif Iqbal, G.W. Johnson, J.N. Graham, R.B. Elms, R.A. Woolmer, M.H. Denness (captain), A.G.E. Ealham, M.C. Cowdrey, A.P.E. Knott. Kent finished fourth in the County Championship with 4 wins, 3 defeats and 13 draws and achieved their first one-day double of the Benson & Hedges Cup (by beating Worcestershire at Lord's) and the John Player Sunday League (for the second successive season).

Alan Ealham was born in Ashford in 1944 and he represented the county between 1966 and 1982, during which time he played 305 matches. As a right-handed, middle-order batsman he accumulated 10,996 runs (av. 27.62) and of his 7 centuries the best was 153 versus Worcestershire at Canterbury in 1979. He also took 3 wickets (av. 63.00), with a best performance of 1 for 1, and held 175 catches, usually in the covers. He later acted as assistant coach of the county club.

The official souvenir programme for the Gillette Cup final between Kent and Lancashire at Lord's on Monday 9 September 1974. The match had been scheduled for Saturday 7 September but had been abandoned due to bad weather that day.

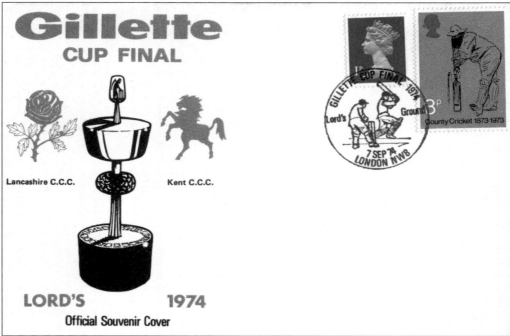

A first day cover produced by Stamp Publicity of Worthing to celebrate the 1974 Gillette Cup final, in which Kent beat Lancashire by 4 wickets.

Kent CCC, 1974. From left to right, back row: C.C. Page (manager), A.G.E. Ealham, R.A. Woolmer, R.B. Elms, J.N. Graham, G.W. Johnson, D. Nicholls, C. Lewis (scorer). Front row: M.C. Cowdrey, Asif Iqbal, B.W. Luckhurst, M.H. Denness (captain), D.L. Underwood, J.N. Shepherd, A.P.E. Knott. Kent finished tenth in the County Championship with 5 wins, 8 defeats and 7 draws. During the season they made a record 427 for 8 declared against Cambridge University at Fenner's and Colin Cowdrey hit 105 versus the touring Pakistanis at Canterbury (added 145 for the third wicket with David Nicholls in the process). Kent won the Gillette Cup for the second time when Lancashire were again defeated at Lord's.

Asif Iqbal made his first-class debut for Hyderabad in 1959/60. He came to the attention of Kent in 1967 after going out to bat with Pakistan on 65 for 8 versus England at The Oval in the final Test of the series and hitting 146 – the highest innings by a number 9 batsman in a Test Match at that time. He was capped by Kent in 1968, his debut season, and in 1971 he scored 1,379 runs (av. 39.40). In total he played 243 matches for Kent, scoring 13,231 runs (av. 37.06) including 26 hundreds. His highest score was 171 versus Gloucestershire at Folkestone in 1978 and he also took 73 wickets (av. 28.71) and held 168 catches. Asif captained Kent in 1977 when they were crowned joint Champions and again between 1981 and 1982. He made 58 Test appearances (6 as captain) and scored 3,575 runs for Pakistan, his 11 centuries including 175 versus New Zealand at Dunedin in 1972/73. He also took 53 wickets with a best performance of 5 for 48 versus New Zealand at Wellington in 1964/65. In 1977 he joined World Series cricket and after retiring in 1982 he was involved in the establishment of cricket in Sharjah.

Kent CCC, 1977. Kent finished in equal first place in the County Championship, sharing the title with Middlesex and so achieving the county's sixth success in the competition. They finished the season with 9 wins, 2 defeats and 10 draws. From left to right, back row: C. Lewis (scorer), B.W. Luckhurst, N.J. Kemp, C.J.C. Rowe, R.W. Hills, K.B.S. Jarvis, C.J. Tavaré, P.R. Downton, C.C. Page (manager). Front row: R.A. Woolmer, D. Nicholls, D.L. Underwood, A.G.E. Ealham (captain), G.W. Johnson, J.N. Shepherd, Asif Iqbal.

Paul Downton represented Kent between 1977 and 1979 in 45 matches before he moved to Middlesex in 1980. A wicketkeeper, middle-order right-handed batsman and occasional off-break bowler, his career took off when Alan Knott joined Kerry Packer and in 1977/78 he toured Pakistan and New Zealand as understudy to Bob Taylor. While with Kent (the county of his birth in 1957 and where he schooled before being educated at Exeter University) he scored 396 runs (av. 11.31) with a top score of 31 not out and took 97 catches and 12 stumpings. He played 30 Tests for England. An eye injury, caused by a flying bail while keeping wicket for Middlesex against Hampshire in 1990, prematurely ended his career. His best batting season was 1987 when he hit 1,120 runs (av. 37.33) with a top score of 126 not out.

Kent CCC, 1976. From left to right, back row: J.C.T. Page (manager), C.J.C. Rowe, R.B. Hills, R.A. Woolmer, K.B.S. Jarvis, G.W. Johnson, R.B. Elms, A.G.E. Ealham, C. Lewis (scorer). Front row: D. Nicholls, J.N. Graham, D.L. Underwood, M.H. Denness (captain), B.W. Luckhurst, Asif Iqbal, A.P.E. Knott. Kent finished fourteenth in the County Championship with 5 wins, 7 defeats and 8 draws. For the second successive season they achieved the one-day double of the Benson & Hedges Cup (beating Worcestershire at Lord's in the final) and the John Player Sunday League (winning the competition for the third time).

Kent CCC, 1978. From left to right, back row: C. Lewis (scorer), B.W. Luckhurst, N.J. Kemp, C.J.C. Rowe, R.B. Hills, K.B.S. Jarvis, C.J. Tavaré, P.R. Downton, G.S. Clinton, J.C.T. Page (manager). Front row: R.A. Woolmer, D. Nicholls, D.L. Underwood, A.G.E. Ealham (captain), G.W. Johnson, J.N. Shepherd, Asif Iqbal. Kent finished first in the County Championship, winning it for the seventh time (it was the second time that the Championship had been achieved in successive seasons – the previous occurrence being in 1909 and 1910) with 13 wins, 3 defeats and 6 draws. Derek Underwood took 9 for 32 in an innings versus Surrey at The Oval. Kent beat Derbyshire at Lord's to achieve their third Benson & Hedges Cup success.

Graeme Clinton was born in Sidcup in 1953 and represented the county between 1974 and 1978. As a left-handed top-order batsman he scored 1,142 runs (av. 24.29) with a top score of 88. His right-arm medium-pace bowling took 2 wickets (av. 4.50) with a best performance of 2 for 8 and he held 10 catches. He moved on to Surrey.

M.C. Cowdrey, F.E. Woolley and L.E.G. Ames, each of whom who scored 100 hundreds in first-class cricket during their careers.

Vic Lewis Celebrity XI pictured at St Lawrence during the benefit match against Alan Knott's Kent XI in 1976.

Alan Knott (left player) and Vic Lewis the jazz band leader signing autographs for young supporters after the toss in the benefit match.

Kent and Middlesex players and officials with HRH the Duke of Edinburgh at Buckingham Palace in 1977 with the County Championship Trophy (which was shared by the two counties).

Born in Bromley in 1956, Nick Kemp represented the county between 1977 and 1981, playing 13 matches. He scored 89 runs (av. 8.09) with a top score of 23 and took 12 wickets (av. 51.75) with a best haul of 6 for 119. He later represented Middlesex in 5 matches in 1982.

A tall, aggressive right-arm fast bowler and left-handed late-order batsman, Graham 'Picca' Dilley played for Dartford CC and worked as a diamond setter in Hatton Garden prior to making his Kent debut in 1977 against Cambridge University at Fenner's. He impressed in his first Championship match, taking 5 for 32 versus Middlesex at Lord's. Making 26 Test appearances for England, his first of five tours abroad was to Australia in 1978/79. He played 109 matches for Kent, taking 257 wickets (av. 27.80) with a best performance of 6 for 57, and scored 993 runs (av. 12.89) with a top score of 81. Capped by Kent in 1980, he also represented Natal when he took 7 for 63 versus Transvaal at Johannesburg. During the epic Headingley Test of 1981, Graham hit 56 runs while helping Ian Botham to an eighth wicket partnership of 117 versus Australia. He took 133 Test wickets (av. 28.48) with 6 for 38 versus New Zealand at Christchurch in 1987/88 being his best performance. He moved to Worcestershire in 1987 and played for a rebel England XI in South Africa in 1989/90.

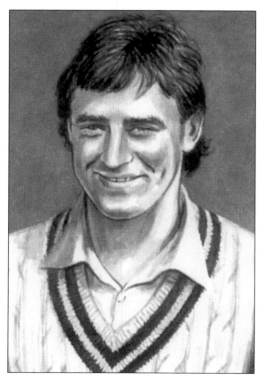

Chris ' Cow' Cowdrey, the eldest of Colin Cowdrey's three sons, was a right-hand middle-order batman and right-arm medium-pace bowler as well as being a fine fielder. He made his Kent debut in 1977 and was capped in 1979, later joining Glamorgan for one season before retiring in 1992. In total he scored 12,202 runs (av. 31.85) with a top score of 159 versus Surrey at Canterbury in 1985 and he took 200 wickets (av. 39.81) with a best performance of 5 for 46 versus Hampshire at Canterbury in 1986. He held a total of 290 catches. Chris captained Kent from 1985 to 1990 and had a single game as England skipper versus West Indies at Headingley in 1990 before suffering an injury. This was only the second father/son captaincy double for England (Frank and George Mann being the first). He toured abroad once to India and Sri Lanka in 1984/85 and played 6 Tests, scoring 101 runs (av. 14.42) with a top score of 38 versus India at Delhi and taking 4 wickets (av. 77.25) with a best performance of 2 for 65 versus India at Madras. He toured South Africa in 1989/90 with the unoffical England XI.

Making his debut in 1974, Chris Tavaré played 259 matches for Kent, scoring 14,201 runs (av. 37.97), including 29 centuries, and holding 269 catches before departing to Somerset in 1989. Educated at Sevenoaks School and Oxford University – where he gained a degree in Zoology and Blues in 1975, 1976 and 1977 – he made his first century (124) against Nottinghamshire at Canterbury in 1977. A right-handed number 3 batsman, he played the anchor-role but was also a stylish stroke-maker. Chris made his Test debut versus West Indies in 1980 when he scored 82 not out at Headingley. In 1981 he scored the slowest Test match 50 in England and also the quickest 100 (off only 27 balls in the Lambert & Butler floodlit match at Selhurst Park). He made a total of 31 Test appearances, scoring 1,753 runs (av. 33.07), including a top score of 149 versus India at Delhi in 1981/82. He captained Kent from 1984 to 1988, when he led them to two losing Lord's finals. He scored 1,430 runs (av. 42.05) in his last season with the county, when he helped them to finish within a single point of the County Championship title. He went on to captain Somerset.

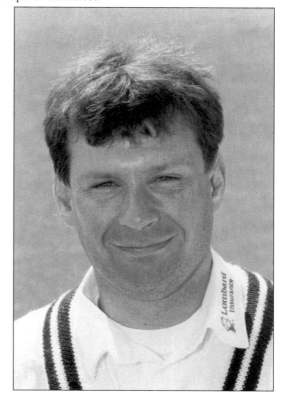

A right-handed top-order batsman and occasional off-break bowler, Neil Taylor scored 110 and 11 on his debut against the touring Sri Lankans at Canterbury in 1979. He was capped in 1982 and went on to represent the county until 1995. His highest innings for Kent was 204 against Surrey in 1990 and his best bowling 2 for 20 versus Somerset in 1985: both were achieved at Canterbury. He moved to Sussex in 1997 and on his debut he recorded 127 versus Northamptonshire at Hove.

Six

From Benson to
the Spitfires

Born at Willesborough, Richard 'Elly' Ellison was a well-built right-arm fast-medium bowler and left-handed batsman. He completed his studies at Tonbridge School and Exeter University before making his Kent debut in 1981 versus Hampshire at Canterbury and was awarded his county cap in 1983. His highest score was 108 versus Oxford University at the University Parks in 1984 and his best bowling performance was 7 for 33 versus Warwickshire at Tunbridge Wells in 1991. He made the first of his 11 Test appearances against West Indies at the Oval in 1984 and he scored 202 Test runs (av. 13.46) with a top score of 41 versus Sri Lanka at Lord's in 1984. He also took 35 wickets (av. 29.94), with a best performance of 6 for 77 versus Australia at Edgbaston in 1985. With Greg Thomas he shares England's highest tenth-wicket stand in the West Indies of 72 at Port-of-Spain in 1984/85. In 1986/87 he represented Tasmania in the Sheffield Shield. His brother, C.C. Ellison, represented Cambridge University between 1981 and 1986 and his grandfather was secretary of Derbyshire CCC in 1915.

The son of William, an Australian Rules footballer, Terry 'Clem' Alderman was nicknamed after a former Brisbane Lord Mayor and made his first-class debut in 1974/75 for Western Australia when he took 5 for 65 against New South Wales at Sydney. He was a deceptive right-arm medium-pace bowler best suited to English conditions and represented Australia in 41 Tests, making his debut in 1981 and taking 170 wickets (av. 27.15) with a best haul of 6 for 47 versus England at Brisbane in 1990/91. At his best against England, he toured twice in 1981 and 1989 when he accumulated a total of 83 Test wickets. In 1984 he took 76 wickets (av. 22.69) for Kent and returned in 1986 to take a further 98 (av. 19.20) including 8 for 46 versus Derbyshire at Derby. In 1988 he represented Gloucestershire and from only three seasons in county cricket amassed 249 wickets (av. 21.35). He was a fine slip fieldsman and a modest late-order batsman, with a top score of 52 not out versus Sussex at Hastings in 1984.

Born in Antigua in 1960, Eldine Baptiste represented Kent between 1981 and 1987, playing 87 matches for the county. An attractive all-rounder, he scored 3,195 runs (av. 29.85) with a top score of 136 not out versus Yorkshire at Abbeydale Park in Sheffield in 1983 and he took 218 wickets (av. 28.46) with a best haul of 8 for 76.

Kent CCC, 1994. From left to right, back row: M.M. Patel, S.C. Willis, N.W. Preston, J.B. Thompson, D.W. Spencer, M.J. Walker. Middle row: F. Errington (physiotherapist), J.C. Foley (scorer), T.R. Ward, D.P. Fulton, T.M. Wren, M.J. McCague, D.W. Headley, N.J. Llong, M.V. Fleming, M.A. Ealham, A.G.E. Ealham (director of youth coaching), D. Foster (coach). Front row: C. Penn, G.R. Cowdrey, C.L. Hooper, M.R. Benson (captain), S.A. Marsh, R.M. Ellison, N.R. Taylor, A.P. Igglesden.

A reliable, stocky, left-handed opening batsman and occasional off-break bowler, Mark Benson was born in Shoreham in 1958 and he represented the county in 261 matches between 1980 and 1993. Scoring 16,845 runs (av. 41.49), his highest score was 257 versus Hampshire at Southampton in 1991. He captained the county between 1991 and 1993, inbetween the reigns of Christopher Cowdrey and Steve Marsh. He also served Kent as coach and is now an ECB umpire on the county circuit.

Chris Penn was born in Dover in 1963 and played for Kent as a right-arm medium-fast bowler and useful late-order, left-handed batsman. He represented the county in 127 matches between 1982 and 1993, scoring 2,048 runs (av. 18.78), taking 295 wickets (av. 33.18) and holding 56 catches. His highest score was 115 versus Lancashire at Old Trafford and his best bowling performance was 7 for 70. Since retiring he has been an ECB cricket development officer for Kent and is based in Sandwich.

Paul Farbrace played 8 matches for the county between 1987 and 1989, prior to joining Middlesex who he represented until 1996. He scored 193 runs (av. 21.44), with a highest score of 75 not out, held 18 catches and made 2 stumpings.

Left: A right-handed, top-order batsman and occasional right-arm slow bowler, Trevor Ward represented the county between 1986 and 1999. He made his debut for Kent against Hampshire at Southampton and was capped in 1989. His highest score for the county was 235 not out versus Middlesex at Canterbury in 1991 and his best bowling performance was 3 for 20 versus Glamorgan at Canterbury in 1990. The 1999 season was his last with the county – with only 139 runs (av. 11.58) and a top score of 42 in 7 championship matches to his name, he was not retained and moved to Leicestershire for the 2000 season. *Right:* Graham Cowdrey, son of M.C. and brother of C.S., was born in Farnborough in 1964. A right-handed, middle-order batsman and right-arm, medium-pace bowler he made his Kent debut in 1984 having schooled at Tonbridge and Durham University. He was capped in 1988 and recorded his highest score four seasons later in 1992 when he hit 147 versus Gloucestershire at Bristol. He retired from county cricket in 1998.

First day cover produced by Benham of Folkestone to celebrate the issue of the summertime set of stamps, which included the 35p stamp of Lord's. The cover, posted at Canterbury on 2 August 1994, depicts a picture of the Kent versus Lancashire match at Canterbury in 1906.

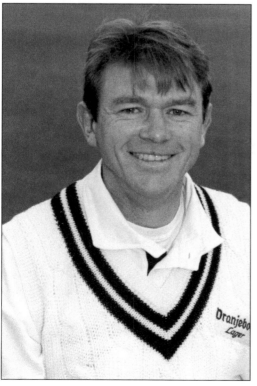

Top left: Son of county stalwart Alan, Mark Ealham was born in 1969. He made his county debut against Lancashire at Old Trafford in 1989. Since then, the right-handed, middle-order batsman and medium-pace bowler has become one of the best all-round cricketers on the county circuit. He has played 8 Tests and 20 one-day internationals since making his debut in 1996. *Top right:* Born in Guyana in 1966, Carl Hooper played 60 Tests and was one of the most talented batsman to grace county and Test cricket. A right-hand batsman and right-arm bowler, he was also an excellent fieldsman, particularly at second slip and backward point. Kent signed Hooper after his successful 1991 tour of England. Hooper became only the second player (Sir Learie Constantine being the first) to hit a ball clear over the lime tree within the outfield at Canterbury. *Left:* Born in Newhaven in 1961, Alan Wells made his Kent debut against Derbyshire at Canterbury in 1997 having previously represented Sussex. A right-handed batsman and right-arm, medium-pace bowler, he received his county cap in 1997 and made his highest score of 111 versus Gloucestershire at Canterbury in 1999.

Left: Left-arm slow bowler Min Patel made his county debut against Middlesex at Canterbury in 1989. and has been a consistent performer. In 1996 he played 2 Tests for England, having previously toured abroad with England 'A' to India. His best performances to date have been 8 for 96 versus Lancashire at Canterbury in 1994 and 58 not out versus Hampshire at Canterbury in 1998. *Right:* Martin McCague made his first-class debut for Western Australia in 1990/91 and his debut for Kent in 1991 versus Middlesex at Lord's. The Northern Irish right-arm fast bowler and right-handed, late-order batsman has played 3 Tests for England and has toured abroad with both the senior and 'A' squads. His best performances so far have been 9 for 86 versus Derbyshire at Derby in 1994 and 63 not out against Surrey at the Oval in 1996.

Left: Son of Ron and grandson of the legendary George, Dean Headley joined Kent in 1993, making his debut versus Zimbabwe 'B' while on tour in Harare. A right-arm, fast-medium pace bowler, he has played over a dozen Tests and one-day internationals for England since 1996. His best performances for Kent so far are 81 runs versus Hampshire in 1998 and 8 for 98 versus Derbyshire at Derby in 1996. *Right:* Right-handed all-rounder Matthew Fleming made his Kent debut against Cambridge University at Fenner's in 1989. He was capped the following season and in 1999 took over the captaincy from Steve Marsh. He played 11 one-day internationals for England in 1997. His best performances to date, both achieved in 1997, are 138 versus Essex at Canterbury and 5 for 51 versus Nottinghamshire at Trent Bridge.

 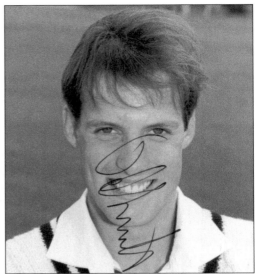

Left: The elder brother of Bryan C. (Mashonaland and Zimbabwe), Paul Strang was born in Bulawayo in 1970. A leg-break and googly bowler he represented Kent in 1997 as the county's overseas player, taking 63 wickets (av. 30.61) with a best performance of 7 for 118 versus Lancashire at Old Trafford. He also hit 82 runs against Leicestershire at Canterbury. Paul's Test performances have included 106 not out against Pakistan at Sheikhupura in 1996/97 and 5 for 106 versus Sri Lanka in Colombo in 1996/97. *Right:* Ed Smith made his Kent debut in 1996 against Derbyshire at Derby aged twenty-one. Educated at Tonbridge School and Cambridge University, where he attained Blues in 1996 and 1997, he has filled one of the opening positions with much promise for the county in the years ahead. So far his best performance for Kent has been 102 versus Hampshire at Portsmouth in 1997. He represented England under-19s in 1996 and was unlucky not to figure on one of England's 1999/2000 winter tours.

Kent CCC, 1996. From left to right, back row: D.W. Spencer, R.J. Key, B.C. Phillips, S.C. Willis, M.J. Walker. Middle row: J. Foley (scorer), F. Errington (physiotherapist), D.P. Fulton, J. Thompson, T.M. Wren, N.W. Preston, A.P. Wells, J.G. Wright (coach), A.G.E. Ealham (director of coaching). Front row: N.J. Llong, M.V. Fleming, P.C. Strang, G.R. Cowdrey, S.A. Marsh (captain), T.R. Ward, A.P. Igglesden, M.J. McCague, M.M. Patel.

Kent CCC, 1998. From left to right, back row: J. Foley (scorer), J.G. Wright (coach), R.J. Key, D.P. Fulton, J. Thompson, B.C. Phillips, M.J. McCague, J. Hockley, E. Stanford, D.C. Masters, M.J. Walker, S.C. Willis, A.G.E. Ealham (director of coaching). Front row: N.J. Llong, M.M. Patel, D.W. Headley, M.V. Fleming, G.R. Cowdrey, S.A. Marsh (captain), T.R. Ward, A.P. Igglesden, A.P. Wells, M.A. Ealham, F. Errington (physiotherapist).

Kent CCC, 1999. From left to right, back row: M.J. Walker, S.C. Willis, D.C. Scott, W. House, M.J. Banes, J. Ford. Middle row: J. Hockley, C. Walsh, D. Masters, B.C. Phillips, R.J. Key, E. Smith, M. Broadhurst. Front row: M.M. Patel, A.P. Wells, S.A. Marsh, T.R. Ward, M.V. Fleming (captain), M.J. McCague, A. Symonds, D.W. Headley, N.J. Llong.

KENT COUNTY CRICKET CLUB

PLAYERS 1999

OFFICIAL AUTOGRAPH SHEET

MATTHEW BANES	**RICHARD CLINTON**	**MARK EALHAM**	**MATTHEW FLEMING** (Captain)
JAMIE FORD	**DAVID FULTON**	**DEAN HEADLEY**	**JAMES HOCKLEY**
WILL HOUSE	**ROBERT KEY**	**NIGEL LLONG**	**STEVE MARSH**
DAVID MASTERS	**MARTIN McCAGUE**	**MINAL PATEL**	**BEN PHILLIPS**
MARTIN SAGGERS	**DARREN SCOTT**	**ED SMITH**	**ANDREW SYMONDS**
JULIAN THOMPSON	**MATTHEW WALKER**	**CHRIS WALSH**	**TREVOR WARD**
	ALAN WELLS	**SIMON WILLIS**	

Kent County Cricket Club autograph sheet for the 1999 season.

Matthew Walker is the ground record holder for the highest individual innings for Kent on the St Lawrence ground at Canterbury with 275 not out against Somerset in 1996. Born in Gravesend in 1974, he made his debut for the county in 1993 versus Zimbabwe 'B' at Harare while on a club tour and has since been a regular member of the First XI. A left-handed batsman and right-arm slow bowler, he captained England at under-19 level between 1992 and 1993 on tours to India, Sri Lanka and the West Indies. In 1999 he scored 450 runs (av. 21.43) with a top score of 93 in the County Championship.

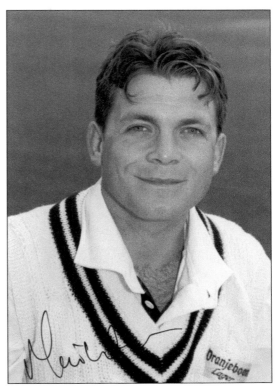

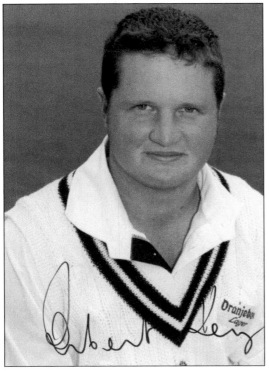

Robert Key was born in East Dulwich in 1979. A right-handed, top-order batsman and off-break bowler he made his county debut in 1998 against Middlesex at Canterbury. Since then he has represented England under-19 and 'A' teams abroad. His best performances so far have been 125 in the County Championship and 76 not out in the CGU Sunday League, both in 1999.

Kent's capped players, 1999. From left to right, back row: M.M. Patel, A.P. Wells, D.W. Headley, M.J. McCague, A. Symonds (overseas player), N.J. Llong. Front row: S.A. Marsh, M.V. Fleming (captain), T.R. Ward.

Kent Spitfires versus England, World Cup warm-up match, 1999. From left to right, back row: R. Croft, J. Thompson, N. Hussain, E. Smith, A. Mullally, A. Symonds, A. Flintoff, R.J. Key, I. Austin, D.A. Scott, N.V. Knight, M.J. Walker. Front row: D.W. Headley, G.P. Thorpe, M.A. Ealham, A.J. Hollioake, M.V. Fleming (captain), A.J. Stewart (captain), T.R. Ward, N.H. Fairbrother, S.C. Willis, D. Gough.

Seven

Grounds of the County

KENT) "MY COUNTY, GENTLEMEN!"

A spectator on the field of play at the Nevill Cricket Ground in 1922. The highest innings total for Kent at the ground was 519 for 6 declared, which was made against Warwickshire in 1928, with the highest individual innings being 214 by J. Seymour versus Essex in 1914.

Kent and All England playing at Canterbury on 4 August 1845. Thirteen years later, in 1858, J. Jackson took 9 for 35 in an innings for the county against England.

Action from the St Lawrence Cricket Ground in 1877 – the year after W.G. Grace had scored the highest individual innings against the county when he made 344 for MCC at the ground.

Cricket being played at St Lawrence in 1905 – a year before Kent recorded their highest innings total at the ground of 568 versus Sussex in 1906. Frank Woolley's 5,279 runs and Tich Freeman's 342 wickets are the records for the highest aggregate number of runs scored and wickets taken for Kent at this venue.

Cricket Ground. St. Lawrence, Canterbury

St Lawrence, viewed by the Pavilion in 1923, looking towards the former Nackington Road Stand (since refurbished and renamed the Les Ames Stand).

The huge Bank Holiday crowd at St Lawrence in August 1928, looking from the Pavilion Annexe towards the lime tree and the Nackington Road end.

Spectators at the cricket being played at St Lawrence in 1930.

The famous lime tree at Canterbury – this is the only instance of a county ground with a tree within the boundary area. This photograph was taken in 1938.

The Frank Woolley Stand and Pavilion, St Lawrence, 1972. Eighteen years later, Canterbury witnessed two record-breaking wicket partnerships, both for and against the county: Simon Hinks and Neil Taylor added 366 for the second wicket versus Middlesex and Darren Bicknell and David Ward added 413 for the third wicket for Surrey against Kent.

An aerial picture of the St Lawrence ground pictured from the east during the Canterbury Festival Week in 1988 with Old Dover Road to the right and Nackington Road to the left of the picture. The famous lime tree can be seen within the playing area together with the Les Ames Stand, Colin Cowdrey Stand, Frank Woolley Stand, Leslie Chiesman Pavilion and

Pavilion Annexe in a clockwise direction from the sightscreen at the Nackington Road end of the ground. During festival week one of the highlights is the collection of marquees and tents that house a variety of local organisations and institutions.

The Angel at Tonbridge in 1906. Kent played 106 matches here between 1869 and 1939 with 53 wins, 36 defeats, 17 draws and 1 abandoned match. The highest innings total recorded on this ground for Kent was 621 for 6 declared versus Essex in 1922. Les Ames' 210 versus Warwickshire in 1933 was the highest individual score for the county at Tonbridge. Colin Blythe took 9 for 30 in an innings here (with match figures of 15 for 76) against Hampshire in 1904. Frank Woolley's 3,159 runs and Tich Freeman's 270 wickets are the highest aggregate number of runs scored and wickets taken for Kent at The Angel.

The pavilion and ground at the Private Bank Sports Ground (Catford) during the Kent versus Gloucestershire match in 1909 when Kenneth Hutchings scored the fastest century for the county in just 50 minutes. Kent played 38 matches at this venue between 1875 and 1921, with 18 wins, 14 defeats and 6 drawn matches.

Higher Cricket Ground, Tunbridge Wells Common, 1920. Kent used the Higher Ground for 28 matches between 1845 and 1884 with 14 wins, 12 defeats and 2 drawn matches.

Kent versus Surrey at the Rectory Field, Blackheath, 1922. Kent played 84 first-class matches at this ground between 1887 and 1971, of which 27 were won, 23 lost and 34 drawn. The highest innings total at this venue was 560 for 6 declared when Colin Cowdrey scored 250 while adding 242 for the fourth wicket with John Pretlove against Essex in 1959.

Kent versus Lancashire at the Bat and Ball Ground, Gravesend, 1923. Kent first visited Gravesend in 1849 and played 143 first-class matches there up until 1971, when the venue ceased being used by the county. Of those matches, 64 were won, 48 lost and 31 drawn. Ken Hutchings and Frank Woolley added 296 for the fourth wicket against Northamptonshire in 1908 and during this particular match Kent attained their highest innings total on the ground of 561 all out.

Crabble Athletic Ground, Dover, 1947. Kent played 106 first-class matches at Dover between 1907 and 1976 with 48 wins, 31 defeats and 27 drawn matches. Bill Ashdown holds the record for the highest individual innings on the ground with 305 not out against Derbyshire in 1935, when Kent achieved a highest innings total of 560 all out. Frank Woolley, with 2,611 runs, has scored the most runs here with A.P. 'Tich' Freeman taking 208 wickets for the county. Kent made their lowest innings total on this ground in 1957 when they were dismissed for just 43 by Middlesex. The lowest opposition score was 44 by Leicestershire in 1912.

124

Cricket being played at Mote Park, Maidstone, 1966. The best bowling performances on the ground for the county were 10 for 131 in an innings by Tich Freeman versus Lancashire in 1929 and 15 for 117 in a match by David Halfyard versus Worcestershire thirty years later in 1959. Laurie Todd and Les Ames added 273 for the second wicket versus Essex in 1947 here and during that match the highest innings total for and against the county on the ground was achieved: 580 for 6 declared by the county and 502 all-out by the visitors. Frank Woolley's 2,897 runs and Tich Freeman's 198 wickets represents the highest aggregate number of runs scored and wickets taken for Kent here.

The main members' pavilion at the Mote Ground in 1984. Both 'for' and 'against' individual batting records on this ground were set during matches with Lancashire. In 1927 Percy Chapman scored 260 for Kent and in 1984 Graeme Fowler scored 226 against the county.

Cricket at Mote Park in 1969, viewed from the bank by the Tabernacle and scoreboard.

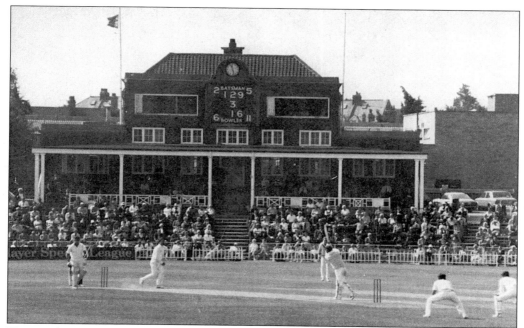

The pavilion at Cheriton Road, Folkestone. Kent played 84 matches at the ground between 1926 and 1991 with 34 wins, 17 defeats and 33 drawn matches. Three ground records were achieved during the match with Gloucestershire in 1933 when Kent recorded their highest innings total of 592 for 5 declared, Les Ames and Laurie Todd added 259 for the third wicket and Les Ames hit a record individual innings of 295.

Cricket at Cheriton Road in 1968. Frank Woolley's 3,525 runs and Tich Freeman's 329 wickets are the highest aggregate of runs scored and wickets taken for Kent on the ground.

The pavilion at the Midland Bank Sports Association Ground, Leonard Road, New Beckenham, Kent. The ground was only used once by Kent, on 10 May 1970, for a John Player Sunday League fixture with Champions Lancashire. The ground was first used for cricket in 1920 and from 1923 was used by Midland Bank. The original pavilion was destroyed by a V-2 rocket in 1945 but was rebuilt after the Second World War and reopened in 1950. The ground is not to be confused with the Lloyds Bank Sports Ground (situated in Copers Cope Road, New Beckenham) which was only used for a single match by the county in June 1954 when the visitors were Gloucestershire.

A Kent county match at Hesketh Park, Dartford, 1976. Kent played 33 first-class matches at Dartford between 1956 and 1990 with 9 wins, 8 defeats and 16 drawn matches. Chris Tavaré holds the record for the highest individual innings on the ground of 150 not out versus Essex in 1985, when Kent achieved a highest innings total of 476 for 9 declared. Alan Ormrod holds the ground record for the highest individual innings against Kent with 204 not out for Worcestershire in 1973, when the visitors achieved the highest total against of 463. Fred Ridgway took 8 for 39 in an innings and 12/101 in the match here against Lancashire in 1960.